How to Catch Trout Between the Hatches

How to Catch Trout Between the Hatches

Jerry Meyer

Charles Scribner's Sons / New York

Photographs on title page, facing page, and the
following page courtesy of Donald W. Pfitzer.
All other photographs are by the author unless
otherwise specified.

Library of Congress Cataloging in Publication Data

Meyer, Jerry, 1939–
   How to catch trout between the hatches.
   Includes index.
   1. Trout fishing. 2. Fly fishing. I. Title.
SH687.M45   799.1'755   82–639
ISBN 0–684–17467–7   AACR2

1 3 5 7 9 11 13 15 17 19 F/C 20 18 16 14 12 10 8 6 4 2

Printed in the United States of America.

To Katherine, the city girl who moved to a cabin at the end of a one-lane dirt road so I could be near mountains and trout

*T*o write a book, especially a book on fly fishing, the author must be supported by many people. It would be impractical to attempt to list all those people who contributed to this volume. A list of those who made the most significant contributions would include Don Pfitzer and Paul Luce, the best two teachers any trout fisherman ever had; Dave Hall, whose patience and editorial skills transformed my manuscript into a book; and Heywood Hosch, Clara Martin, Gary Merriman, Ron Hickman, Ed Zern, Jim Bashline, and Chet Fish.

Contents

How to Catch Trout Between the Hatches

Introduction

HATCH MATCHING has gotten a lot more exposure than it deserves in periodicals and fly-fishing books during the last few decades. Trout feed selectively on mature aquatic insects only about 10 percent of the time, according to surveys of stomach contents done by qualified fishery biologists. The other 90 percent of a trout's food is taken below the surface as the opportunity presents itself. This book was written to provide the reader with a variety of techniques to use during those times when the angler doesn't have a hatch to match.

What I propose are some alternatives to duplicating mature aquatics. You will not need a degree in entomology or a twenty-pound field guide to mayflies to make full use of this book. Nor will you need a supply of space-age materials to tie duplicates of the latest "miracle fly" designed by the author.

A good fisherman must be like an entire good football team, in which depth and versatility are the only keys to consistent success. A team that has only a good running or passing game or is a good specialty team or has good defense is doomed to failure. Likewise, a fly fisherman who devotes the majority of his time to matching adult aquatics is doomed to being successful only during those infrequent times when a hatch is on the water.

I have attempted to avoid "hero stories" about how the author caught specific fish on specific streams and have focused instead on basic concepts that can be applied to many situations. For instance, the chapter on presentation deals with some fundamentals that supersede fancy trick casts if the angler is to be successful.

The purpose of this book is to provide a variety of techniques that are uncomplicated and can be used by the angler of limited experience as well as the fisherman who has already served his apprenticeship: if it makes those nonhatch periods on a stream more successful for you, I have accomplished what I set out to do.

Anatomy of a Trout Stream

THE FIRST TIME I ever looked at a mountain trout stream, it seemed I was gazing at the aquatic equivalent of a lunar landscape. As I stared into the gin-clear waters of Moccasin Creek in the mountains of north Georgia, I could see the entire bottom of the stream, which consisted of nothing more than a few rocks and some gravel. I could see nothing for a fish to eat or any place for one to hide, and thought the creek must be entirely devoid of all forms of life.

Fortunately, my fishing partner and instigator of that first trout-fishing trip was Paul Luce, who had grown up on the trout streams in upstate New York. After listening to all the reasons why I didn't think there could possibly be any fish in those barren-looking waters, Paul studied the stream for a while, then told me to cast above a deep run between a large boulder and an undercut stream bank. I got a strike and landed a rainbow about nine inches long, which could not have surprised me more if it had been a ten-foot hammerhead shark!

Several decades have passed, but I still remember vividly my first erroneous impressions of that little run on Moccasin Creek. Even trout fishermen with a modicum of experience rarely comprehend the importance of understanding the biomass in a trout stream. Because one's first comprehension of the multitude and variety of life forms in a trout stream is so startling, I always schedule an on-stream introduction to capturing nymphs, crustaceans, minnows, and terrestrials early on the agenda at the several trout-fishing schools where I teach. To be a consistently successful trout fisherman, you must first understand the habitat of a trout and be aware of the trout's relationships with all the life forms that share it.

Writing a lengthy dissertation on a single trout stream wouldn't be worth it unless you were going to fish that specific stream, for there is no such thing as a typical trout stream that can be used as a model. Even the same stream can change so drastically in just a few hundred yards that techniques which produced in one place won't work a short distance away.

A stream must provide certain requirements that are necessary for trout to live and thrive. Understanding the needs of a trout and how those needs are satisfied will do more for your ratio of fish caught per hours fished than knowing 500 fly patterns on sight or knowing the Latin names of 1,436 mayflies.

The most obvious component of a trout's world is the stream itself, flowing water that can be both his best friend and his worst foe. To understand streams you need some basic understanding of hydrodynamics, or more specifically hydrokinetics, the science of the theories of the motion of liquids.

Anything that is in motion and makes contact with a stationary obstacle loses velocity. Consequently, any time flowing water comes in contact with a stationary object such as a boulder, log, stream bottoms, or stream banks, velocity is lost. When flowing water comes into contact with something stationary and loses velocity, a cushion of comparatively slower moving water is created. The size of the obstruction and the angle of contact determine how big the cushion is and to what degree the flow of current is retarded.

The effect of obstacles on flowing water can be better understood if we think of a trout stream as being many small streams flowing in close proximity, rather than as one large single current. As a general rule, the current will be strongest in the middle of the stream near the surface, unless there is a midstream obstruction such as a large boulder.

Cushions can also be created in stream-bottom depressions that provide more protection from flowing current than given by any relatively flat area surrounding it.

Trout cannot fight strong currents continuously and survive, so they seek hiding places, or "lies," in cushions that provide them with some refuge from flowing water. Most anglers are aware that a trout can find refuge from flowing water behind a midstream obstacle such as a boulder, but many neglect the cushion that is present in *front* of the object. As flowing water strikes the obstruction, pressure builds up and a wedge-shaped cushion is created, in which the current is reduced enough to provide respite for the fish.

Such physical and geographical features as water depth and velocity, bottom configuration, stream course or route, type of stream bank, rate of drop in elevation, and in-stream obstacles occur together in various ways to create the basic conditions that limnologists use to describe streams, pools, flats, riffles, runs, rapids, and cascades. Each of these various stream properties plays an important role in the survival and well-being of trout. Pools and deep runs provide security and refuge from flowing water, rapids and cascades aerate the water so that it maintains a high dissolved-oxygen content, and riffles serve as the primary food-producing habitat in most streams.

In addition to flowing water and the physical properties of the stream itself, another component—streamside vegetation—greatly influences the life-style of trout and their relationship to a stream. Streamside vegetation can provide shelter, terrestrial food items, and even refuge from flowing water, around fallen trees. Even after an old tree stump has long rotted out and all remnants of the tree have been flushed away, the root holes provide prime protective cover for trout.

A large spring flows out of the side of the mountain near my home. Several years ago I placed a few trout in a pool in the small stream created by the spring, to do some close-up photography. The small pool seemed an ideal habitat, since it was about thirty feet by twenty feet across and ranged in depth from about ten to eighteen inches. I placed four trout each about ten inches long in the pool and gave them a few days to settle down and acclimate to their new surroundings before returning to shoot pictures.

You can imagine how surprised I was when I returned to find the pool completely barren of trout. It was physically impossible for a trout to have left the pool at either end, since it was bounded by a small waterfall on the upstream side and a dam I had built at the lower end that allowed only an inch or two of water to flow over the top. A closer examination revealed that all four trout had secluded themselves in old root holes running into the stream bank. In each case, the holes were large enough that the fish just barely fit inside. These were hatchery fish, so you can imagine how frequently a wary wild trout must take advantage of such cover.

One further component of the trout's environment, security, cannot be overemphasized, since it is the primary requirement for survival and is at the top of a trout's priority list. Even before a trout hatches from an egg, it is susceptible to being devoured by larger prey. Its entire life must be spent on the alert to avoid being consumed by ospreys, kingfishers, otters, mink, water snakes, and fish larger than himself. Those that are to survive long enough to reach catchable proportions must make a career out of being wary.

Because lies that provide easy access to food and security simultaneously are greatly favored by trout, such locations are most frequently occupied by the largest and most aggressive fish. Big browns show a decided preference for prime lies such as those that have overhead cover of some sort like a fallen log or an undercut bank or a rock ledge that creates a small underwater cave.

To obtain trophy proportions a trout must have four things. In his genetic pool he must possess the inherited characteristics from his parents to grow to a large size. He must have a habitat that is conducive to obtaining a large size. He must have time to reach his full growth potential. And finally he must possess a highly sensitive awareness which sends him dashing to cover when he detects anything suspicious in his environment. It is this last characteristic of trophy fish which prevents the casual angler who practices sloppy presentation, reckless wading technique and incautious approach from ever catching a trout of bragging size proportions.

A trout stream must also provide cold, oxygen-rich water. Brook trout cannot tolerate water temperatures over 65 degrees F., although browns and rainbows can tolerate slightly higher temperatures. For browns the minimum dissolved-oxygen content at 68 degrees F. is approximately 5 parts per million. Browns grow best and are most active between 65 and 75 degrees F. but have been known to tolerate temperatures as high as 81 for short periods of time. As a knowledgeable fishery biologist once told me, "It is the extremes that kill trout, not the averages, when it comes to water temperatures and dissolved oxygen."

The trout's preference for cooler waters becomes important to fishermen when water temperatures become marginal during the hot days and low waters of late summer. Trout will seek cooler waters during these periods and can often be found congregated at the confluence of a large stream and a spring-fed tributary. This pattern of behavior is more pronounced in freestone streams (discussed in a moment) which are more susceptible to surface and air temperature changes, than limestone streams, which are fed primarily by subterranean water sources and remain fairly consistent in temperature all year round.

Although there is no average trout stream, there are two major types of trout streams into which most waters can be categorized: limestone or chalk, and freestone. These two types of streams have some major differences of which the angler must be aware, in order to plan his techniques accordingly.

Limestone streams are frequently called spring creeks, usually in error, since limestone streams are normally the upper surface of a huge subterranean reservoir that extends above the surface in depressions at relatively low elevations. They are merely underground rivers that have water levels higher than the surrounding ground levels. In essence, limestone streams are the upper tip of a huge underground reservoir comparable to the tip of a big melted iceberg. Since the portion of the reservoir above the surface is just a small fraction of the entire water mass, a limestone stream is not appreciably influenced by surface temperature or other climatic changes. With few exceptions, most of our limestone streams are located in Pennsylvania, Montana, Idaho, Wyoming, Michigan, and Wisconsin.

Freestone streams, on the other hand, usually have their source at higher elevations and are fed by true springs, snow melt, and the runoff of surface water. This is conducive to rapid fluctuations in water flow and temperature. A heavy rainstorm or sudden snow melt can create flash floods that can scour a streambed, devastating aquatic food sources, destroying trout eggs, trout fry, and even killing mature fish. These same surface waters can at times deposit silt in sufficient quantities to smother trout eggs and aquatic insect forms. The presence of silt in even small amounts can create enough turbidity to cause trout to stop feeding for days at a time.

Freestone streams are the most common, which is unfortunate, since limestone streams are more fertile and more consistent in water temperature and volume. Not only do trout living in limestone streams have the benefit of consistent water temperature and volume, they also have less turbidity to contend with. But probably the greatest advantage of limestone streams is their high fertility, caused by the presence of dissolved limestone, calcium carbonate, and other nutrients. This fertility generates phenomenal growth in one-celled plant and animal forms, which in turn stimulate growth in the entire food chain, eventually producing massive trout populations. As a result of chalk streams' high fertility, they can produce and sustain more pounds of trout than can a freestone stream. A fertile limestone stream can be expected to produce approximately 250 pounds of trout per acre per year, whereas a freestone stream could be expected to produce only about 50 pounds per acre per year.

To really appreciate the importance of limestone stream fertility and its impact on trout production, it is important to understand how the food chain functions. First are the producers, including all plants, algae, and plankton. Through the process of photosynthesis these producers combine sunlight, nutrients, and carbon dioxide to form carbohydrates. These carbohydrates are then consumed by the next stratum in the chain, which consists of insect larvae and pupae, fish fry, snails, and minute forms of insects. The next stratum consists of foragers such as panfish, sculpins, dace, chubs, and crayfish. The fourth level in the food chain includes trout and other predators. Bacteria also play an important role throughout the food chain, as they recycle decaying vegetation and other organic material.

A general rule of thumb can be applied to determine how much food is required to produce and support each stratum in the food chain. For every thousand pounds of producers, you can expect one hundred pounds of consumers, ten pounds of foragers, and one pound of predators. The five-pound trout you catch is the net result of five thousand pounds of producers on the lower end of the food chain.

Once you understand the food chain and what is required to sustain a trout, it is easy to see why the wholesale dumping of trout into a stream is not the solution to low trout populations. Habitat management and stream improvements are the only way we can ever hope to maintain or improve the trout fishing we now have.

To reproduce naturally, trout require specific conditions. A successful hatch depends upon many factors, including consistent volume of water flow with minimal turbidity, coarse gravel to provide protection for eggs and newly hatched fry, and an absence of pollutants. Many of our streams can no longer provide these requirements because of the encroachment of industrial pollution, the use of pesticides, and unrestricted timber harvesting. Any one of these three hazards, plus a multitude of others, can cause natural reproduction in a trout stream to cease completely.

A few trout streams have been created since the turn of the century. The construction of hydroelectric plants has formed large, deep reservoirs that allow water to cool down sufficiently to produce cold-water tailwaters below dams. Many streams that were too warm to support trout suddenly became too cold below dams to maintain bass, panfish, and catfish. These warm-water species have since been replaced by trout, producing some excellent trout fishing.

2/

These midges, not visible on the stream, were discovered by sweeping a terrestrial net through streamside vegetation.

What Trout Eat and How They Eat It

A PARTIAL LIST of what trout eat includes the following:

earthworms	fish eggs	snails
salamanders	baby ducks	leaf hoppers
nymphs	moths	tree hoppers
spiders	frogs	whole kernel corn
mayflies	other trout	crickets
sculpins	dobson flies	grasshoppers
caddis flies	crane flies	gnats
dace	alder flies	house flies
cress bugs	bees	crayfish
caterpillars	fairy shrimp	cheese
ants	freshwater prawns	damselflies
stoneflies	yellow jackets	dragonflies
midges	deer flies	hemlock needles
mice	wasps	

These parts of a trout's diet, not listed in order of importance, obviously include some large morsels that could be consumed only by trout approaching epic proportions. (One survey of rainbow trouts' stomach contents even found a 7.1-inch trout that contained two snakes whose combined total length was over three times that of the trout that had eaten them!) I added the hemlock needles because one study revealed that in twenty-two rainbow trout stomachs out of 241 stomachs examined, hemlock needles and small bits of wood were present. Of the 3,878 recognizable food items contained in the 241 stomachs, the most important foods were (in descending order) various terrestrial insects, caddisfly larvae, mayfly nymphs, and two winged fly larvae. These four categories comprised 84.4 percent of the total. Adult aquatic insects (7.7 percent) and stonefly nymphs (4.5 percent) were next in order of importance.

Immature aquatic insects, crayfish, and mollusks formed 58.9 percent of the total number of food items, indicating that the rainbows examined were primarily subsurface feeders. Adults of aquatic insects comprised only 7.7 percent of the total food items.*

In a lake environment the primary food sources might include scuds, cress bugs, freshwater shrimp, damselflies, dragonflies, midges, mosquito larvae, snails, and leeches.

To say specifically what trout feed on is risky business. The only way you can be sure what a trout is eating is to look in his stomach, and then you are only sure about what that one fish has been eating. At best, a stomach contents survey reveals only what individual trout have eaten at a specific time of year in a particular stream or lake. Determining what trout are feeding on at any specific time and place is at best an educated guess taking into consideration such factors as samples of various food organisms from below the surface, on the surface, and in the surrounding terrestrial habitat. Only after you have established some possible food items can you begin the process of elimination for the various patterns in your fly box.

The biggest mistake a fly fisherman can make is to get locked in to a few favorite fly patterns or fishing techniques that have produced well under certain circumstances and expect them to produce consistently. Only the fisherman adaptable to changes in trout feeding patterns will be consistently successful—the same technique that produced one weekend may not work at all on the same stream a week later.

Trout have two basic feeding patterns: selective and opportunistic. Many excellent books by master fly fishermen on selective-feeding fishing techniques have gone to great detail to identify the exact food organisms trout feed on and how to imitate them. Anyone who denies that trout feed selectively just doesn't have enough experience to

* This survey was made by L. B. Tebo, Jr., and W. W. Hassler on streams in western North Carolina, but similar surveys have probably been made in your own area. The data may be available in state game and fish publications.

make an objective decision. But I also feel that there are some fishermen who have too much experience, which has been overly influenced by preconceived ideas. At best, the most accurately tied flies merely create realistic impressions, rather than being exact duplicates as some contend. If the only thing that caught trout was a perfect replica of a natural food organism, how can we account for all those trout caught on fly patterns that don't look like anything in a trout stream?

There are times when using flies that make realistic impressions is the only way to catch fish, but I also believe that you must take into account that a trout takes the greatest portion of its food below the surface, which is not where you find the adults that so many anglers spend 99 percent of their time trying to duplicate exactly.

What many anglers may fail to take into account is that trout sometimes feed selectively on something other than adult aquatic insects. I am convinced that this type of selective feeding pattern is the most ignored trout behavior. On more than one occasion I have seen a fisherman frantically working a butterfly net to catch a sample of some food organism that selectively feeding trout have locked onto. He has correctly deduced that the fish are feeding selectively but has erroneously assumed that because they are doing so they can be taking only mature aquatic insects that must be absolutely duplicated with a dry fly. It is a biological fact that trout feed on subsurface material in an opportunistic manner the greatest majority of the time. Unless there is evidence that they have temporarily deviated from that behavior and are indeed feeding selectively on adults floating on the surface, you should first direct your attention below the surface.

I have read and listened to horror stories about fishermen who matched the hatch with a size 24 pattern fished on a twelve-foot leader when the water was covered with naturals and fish were rising everywhere. If the leader was twelve feet long and the rod was a mere seven and a half feet, that's twenty feet, even if the fisherman didn't have any fly line through the tip guide. I would have the very devil of a time keeping up with a fly this small if it was a duplicate of hundreds of naturals that were covering the water—I can't even see a size

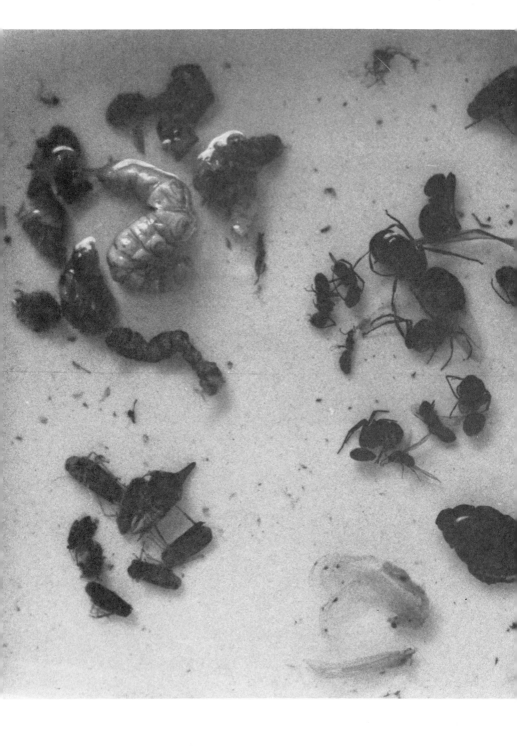

The variety of food organisms found in the stomachs of four trout taken from the same stream during late summer.

24 pattern twenty feet away on my living room carpet! I have taken some of these tiny flies out of my fly box and lost them before I could get them tied onto my tippet. I would rather butcher gnats for hides and tallow than try to fish under such conditions.

Food preferences and feeding habits vary with age and habitat, and these variations can further be influenced by the availability of food organisms. A thunderstorm may cause a minor flash flood that will move gravel and small stones, dislodging and injuring bottom-dwelling nymphs, trout fry, and eggs. But that same shower may flush various terrestrials such as beetles, ants, grasshoppers, and caterpillars into the stream to become fare for hungry trout.

The seasons of the year can have a major effect on what trout eat, since various food organisms are more populous or more readily available at certain times because of their vulnerability during given stages of their development. Terrestrials gain in importance during mid- to late summer as their numbers increase. Emerging nymphs are more vulnerable when they leave the relative security of stream-bottom cover to travel toward the surface through open water. Knowing the life-cycle of the common food organisms in your favorite trout waters can greatly increase your success ratio, but just knowing when mature aquatic insects will be on the water is not enough. How many times have they hatched the day before you were on the stream and the day after you left? Projected hatch times are certainly important, but you should also be aware of other possibilities.

I am convinced, like many other anglers, that really big trout usually feed very late in the day, at night, and early in the morning. Large browns seem to have a decided preference for night feeding, with only two exceptions: feeding during a massive salmonfly hatch on a western stream, and in periods of rainy weather. I have often wondered whether these fish feed at night because they are big—or they got to be big fish because they habitually feed at night.

Night-feeding fish are not to be thought of as those that suffer from lack of motivation, for many food organisms are most active and therefore most available at night. Some green drake hatches run on into the night, and several others, such as the large burrowing mayflies, are night flyers. On more than one occasion I have witnessed various forms of mayflies ovipositing after dark on a rain-slick high-way paralleling a trout stream; apparently the wet highway looked like a stream to the egg-laden females.

Crayfish, moths, and several of the large beetles are nocturnal and no doubt add considerable bulk to a night-feeding trout's midnight buffet. On more than one occasion I have been driven into my tent and under a mosquito net after finishing dinner in camp.

Even after you have correctly determined that a fish is feeding selectively and are as sure as you can realistically be about exactly which organism he is feeding on, or you have observed a fish feeding opportunistically on surface or subsurface food items, your efforts may still produce only frustration. Often an angler may be casting a fly that should produce a strike but doesn't. The fish continues to feed actively—but won't take a fly. This happens to all of us, and, too often, failure to get a feeding fish to strike is blamed on inability to match the hatch. More often than not, I suspect, failure can be at-tributed to casting at the wrong place at the wrong time. This stra-tegic error is caused by the angler's not understanding the factors affecting the mechanics of how a trout takes his food: The pattern varies.

When he has a choice, a trout will usually position himself on what's referred to as a feeding station, which offers some refuge from flowing water but allows him to be close enough to a substantial current to observe food organisms suspended in or floating on the water. He may be holding behind an obstruction such as a boulder or in a depression in the bottom, in an undercut bank, or in a back-current eddy that has no visible obstruction but still produces reduced current flow that does not require excessive expenditures of energy while the feeding fish awaits his stream-borne groceries. Do not ne-glect the wedge of reduced current in front of a boulder; the cushion of slower moving water there may produce a hold for a feeding trout.

The ideal feeding station combines not only refuge from flowing water and easily accessible food in nearby flowing water but also security, in the form of cover such as a large boulder, stream bank, or log, from the trout's enemies. The fish will lie next to this cover, which affords him some protection. When he can get it, his first choice is a feeding station with overhead cover. Such a location is often occupied by the largest fish around, which he will defend against lesser fish that would trespass on his prime station. A location that provides not only refuge from fast water but also is a feeding station and gives security is often called a prime lie. The angler who learns to identify these and constantly stays on the alert for them will probably experience a noticeable increase in the average size of the fish he takes.

In many cases, it is more important to locate the feeding stations than to know exactly what fish are eating. Even if a trout is feeding selectively, it won't do any good to position the right fly in the wrong place.

In a stream, the water moves and the feeding fish pretty much stay in one place. In a lake, the water stays still and the fish move. When fishing in still water you can try to anticipate the approximate route of any feeding fish you observe and cast to where you think he is headed, or else you can fish the water by casting randomly in the approximate vicinity where feeding fish are working.

Beginning fishermen get a jolt of adrenaline when they see a fish rise and take something off the surface. The neophyte usually cannot resist the temptation to cast immediately to the exact spot where he saw the fish break the surface. The fish may continue to rise, but anticipation will soon turn to frustration as the tyro fails to get a strike. He will frequently attribute his lack of success to a failure to "match the hatch," but his real problem was that he probably never cast his fly where the feeding fish could even see it.

A fish feeding in moving water comes off his feeding station and drifts downstream with the food item he is considering. This drift may be only a foot or two or may be measured in yards, depending on many factors. A fish in rough, broken water will have to take surface food quickly before it is swept out of sight. A fish in a long, gentle run or large pool may take a deliberate look at anything he is about to take. Or a fish may be competing with others nearby and have to beat them to the food.

The experienced fisherman enjoys the same spurt of adrenaline and anticipation as the beginner, but he has learned to control his reactions. Usually the knowledgeable oldtimer will stop casting and study several rises, to determine where the fish's feeding station is, where the best location would be to place his cast to allow his fly to drift by the trout's feeding station, and where he should position himself to make the cast. The experienced angler who is studying a rising fish is not unlike the wine connoisseur who swirls a glass of wine to enjoy its color and bouquet as he anticipates the pleasure of drinking it. It is hard to resist the "quick draw" cast right at a rising fish as soon as you see him, but patience and observation will result in more strikes.

One of the most common and easiest mistakes to make when observing a feeding fish is to assume he is taking food off the surface because you witnessed a surface disturbance. What looks like a fish feeding on the surface may only be a trout taking emerging nymphs close to the surface or a submerged terrestrial floating just beneath the surface. A nymphing or "bulging" fish usually doesn't actually break the surface film, though he may disturb it slightly. Another clue is the bubbles that a surface-feeding fish usually expels from his gill flaps as a result of the small amount of air he ingested when he picked a fly off the surface. Before you launch a full-scale surface attack with every fly in your box, make sure your quarry is actually feeding on the surface and not coming up off the bottom to take some subsurface sustenance.

Occasionally you will observe the dull flash of a fish feeding well below the surface as he turns to move back upstream to his feeding station. Here again the temptation is great to cast to the exact spot where you saw the fish, but even if you do collect your wits and cast upstream from where you saw the turning fish, it is easy to cast too far downstream and place your fly behind his feeding station, or, even worse, place your fly right on top of him, which could startle him into a case of lockjaw. When planning your cast for a subsurface feeder, don't forget to take into account that it will require some distance and drift for your fly to get down to the depth where you suspect the fish is on station. If you are not sure exactly where the fish is, cast well above any of the several possibilities and don't pick up your line for the next cast until you are sure line, leader, and fly have drifted well out of the fish's field of vision. A drifting line passing over a fish shouldn't put him down or scare him off his feed, but lifting a line off the water right over his head could put you out of business.

3

Many anglers spend most of their time trying to match a hatch in midstream and thus miss out on some prime fishing by not focusing attention on the shoreline, where larger fish may be holding beneath undercut banks or other streamside cover.

How to Read a Stream

THERE WAS A TIME in my life when I had just begun to catch a few trout and considered myself a better than average trout fisherman, almost an expert, with a few tactics that would take fish fairly regularly. I began to sell some magazine articles and meet fishermen and angling writers from all over the country, and learned quickly after fishing with people like Ed Zern, Don Pfitzer, Gary Merriman, Marty Fishbourne, Ed Leonard, and others that this world was full of fishermen who knew a lot more about trout fishing than I did. All the really good trout fishermen I have ever fished with had one thing in common: They rarely tied on a fly or even assembled their rods when first walking up to a strange stream. They used their nymph seines and terrestrial nets, their eyes and their heads before tying on some "wonder fly." Because they were stream readers first, they were also extremely versatile, committed to the single philosophy of figuring out where the fish were and giving them what they wanted.

You can accomplish this goal in one of two ways: either by casting until you accidentally drop a fly in front of a fish that happens to accidentally look like something good for it to eat, or by logically concluding where fish are most likely to be and what foods they have had access to.

From the moment a beginning trout fisherman steps onto his first stream, he starts looking for a rising fish to cast to. Unfortunately, many anglers never progress past this initial stage. Reading a trout stream by looking only for rising fish is like reading a book by its cover; just finding a fish that is eating is not enough.

The two most important components of successful trout fishing are presentation (see Chapter 4) and being able to read a stream. You must understand the physical properties of moving water and its influence on everything that lives in it, learn why trout may be in certain parts of streams, understand the mechanics of how a trout takes his food and how to recognize various rise forms, and remember to include terrestrial habitat in your evaluation of a trout stream. Reading a stream requires more than just using your eyes. Nymph seines, thermometers, and nets for collecting terrestrial insects are all tools that can add immeasurably to your knowledge of a stream.

A trout faces many threats to his survival that take precedence over his starving to death. From the moment he emerges from an egg until he dies, he must be constantly on the alert, ready to dart to safety at the slightest indication that there is a threatening foe nearby. Trout have an inbred instinct not only to avoid danger by fleeing but also to prevent exposure to enemies by remaining under cover as much as possible. Trout rarely move far from protective shelter even when they are actively feeding; if they have a choice, they will feed from a secure position.

Security can take many forms in a trout stream. A vertical surface—the side of a boulder, a log, a rock ledge, a crevice or steep bank—can provide protective cover on at least one side. A deep pool can provide some security from ospreys and kingfishers. But a trout's first choice when it comes to security is what fishermen call overhead cover. With overhead cover, a trout may feel so secure that he becomes oblivious to all that's going on around him. I have seen trout stick just their heads under a small rock ledge with their whole bodies exposed. In this position they would even submit to being touched, until their heads were pulled out from under the overhead cover, when they would bolt like a shot for another shelter.

Once when I was out with a dozen Explorer Scouts, I met a backpacker from Germany on a stream in northern New Mexico. He was wading in a stream that was about thirty feet wide and groping up under the bank with his hands. When I asked what he was doing, he replied in a thick accent that he was fishing for some supper. I thought we had failed to communicate, until he tossed a flopping rainbow up on the bank. He went on to explain that the streams near his home were all private property with no fishing allowed. To be caught on those private trout waters even with just fish hooks in your possession carried a stiff penalty. So he and his buddies would sneak onto the streams and grapple trout from under the banks.

Overhead cover can be created by a log that is not lying flush against the stream bottom, an undercut bank, a rock outcropping, streamside vegetation, or root holes left under a bank after a tree has been washed away. A severe flood on the little stream near my house had once devastated a trout hatchery. After passing it many times while fishing the stream, I noticed a section of eight-inch pipe that had been washed into the streambed, and it occurred to me that that section of pipe would make ideal overhead cover for a trout. It was only a few feet long, so I went over and picked it up to see if it was occupied—and it was! The fish stayed inside until I lifted it above the surface, then he flopped out and back into the stream.

Many fishermen miss some of their best opportunities for catching big fish by wading next to the bank and casting into deep runs and pools in midstream. Most bigger fish will occupy spots up under overhead cover, a lot of which is in the form of undercut stream banks. The overhang doesn't have to be sizable to be attractive to a fish—six or seven inches is plenty.

When trout select attractive underwater real estate, feeding stations are second only to security lies. A feeding station must provide two things for a trout: refuge from flowing water, and accessibility to food in a nearby current flow. The stations can be located behind, beside, or in front of some in-stream obstruction such as a boulder or downed tree. A depression in the stream bottom affords some protection from strong currents and allows the trout to watch the current flowing over his head for drifting food.

An eddy or backcurrent will often collect food items and also provide a reduced current that will not tax a trout's energy. Side cover, such as a vertical bank, will offer some refuge from flowing water for a trout watching faster currents a little farther out in the stream.

The confluence of two feeder streams concentrates food items from

A good example of a prime trout lie with overhead cover. Few fisher-
men would notice it—and others would not fish it—because of the
difficulty in getting a fly past the roots and branches, but such
inconspicuous lies should be sought out and fished.

both streams and will often attract several trout to the same feeding station, or cause several fish to be on feeding stations fairly close together. When there are several fish on the same station, they usually run a little on the small side. Big fish are defensive and very territorial about their feeding stations and will chase off any fish that are small enough to intimidate.

Small slicks in rough, broken water are often created by some feature that retards the current, such as an obstruction or depression in the stream bottom. Such slicks make good feeding stations because a fish in them is almost entirely surrounded by fast-moving water carrying food. Trout on a feeding station of this type are not provided with much opportunity to scrutinize food closely, so they must take it quickly before it is swept downstream.

Occasionally there are the locations called prime lies that provide security, refuge from flowing water, a feeding station—and usually hold prime fish. All prime lies do not have overhead cover, but because so many of them do it is a component that many experienced anglers watch for constantly when reading a stream.

The more inconspicuous a prime lie, the greater its potential for producing an exceptional fish. Contrast, for example, an obvious prime lie such as a deep run in the middle of a stream that flows by an overhanging ledge—a spot that looks so "fishy" that every rookie in the stream will beat it to death—with a small cavern of modest dimensions under a stream bank partially concealed by tree roots or a scraggly limb. No fisherman in his right mind will try to float a fly past such a spot—why, he might get snagged! Indeed he might, by a fish that could be a centerfold in his favorite fishing magazine.

I am as guilty as anyone else of spending too much time fly casting and not enough time trout fishing: After being on a stream for an hour or two, I sometimes turn into a robot that mechanically casts to all the obvious places. This brand of fishing is relaxing and one of the joys of angling, but it is not the way to catch fish in a stream that gets any fishing pressure at all. The unusual fish come out of the unusual places, not that same deep pool in the middle of the stream that every guy who has ever fished the stream has worked for an hour and a half.

Reading a stream should be something you do before every series of casts. Have you ever seen a good-looking patch of water and waded toward it to make a cast, only to scare off a nice fish from a prime lie you should have seen before you ever started wading? You can keep this kind of aggravation to a bare minimum by carefully scrutinizing any water carefully before you wade through it.

It is good not to wade a stream until you must. If streamside conditions permit walking, you can scout a stream more efficiently by walking on the bank than in the stream. If there are any trout at all in the stream (and there must be or you wouldn't be there, right?), you will scare the bejeezers out of some of them, no matter how cautiously you wade. These fish will dart away from you in panic, setting up a chain reaction that will spook other fish ahead of you.

You can read a stream by walking softly along the bank, staying back away from the stream and using streamside cover for concealment whenever possible. Although stealth is important in approaching trout (see Chapter 4, "Presentation"), you can alert a fish just as easily by recklessly wading while trying to read the water.

Being able to recognize sections of a stream that should hold trout is one of the primary requisites for being a successful fly fisherman, simply because you have to fish where the trout are if you are going to catch them. Just being able to locate possible feeding stations, holding water, or a prime lie will go a long way toward improving your catch, but these abilities alone are not enough. You must also learn to be alert for other indicators that not only suggest the presence of trout but also show how you might go about catching them. If the practice of only looking for feeding fish rising on the surface can be compared to reading a book by looking at its cover, then you are only looking at the table of contents of this hypothetical book if you read a stream by merely looking for holding water or feeding stations or places that may be prime lies. Finding holding water will give some indication about where to find what you are seeking but won't give you the detailed information you need.

It is easy to fall into the habit of associating one or two factors with the presence of trout. Several successful experiences with common circumstances will often lock a fisherman on to a "selective fishing pattern" and (just like a trout that is feeding selectively) that angler will fish with the same fly pattern on the same type of water to

When reading big trout waters, think of them as a collection of many small streams flowing in close proximity, and read each current as an individual stream. Photo courtesy Don Pfitzer.

the point of addiction. You have probably met fishermen who are locked into a "selective fishing pattern" and may even be one yourself; perhaps you fish just a few patterns, in just certain types of water. I am not talking about anglers who specialize only in nymph fishing or dry-fly fishing or streamer fishing, who are usually knowledgeable fishermen who have studied a particular form of fly fishing. Although they may fish nothing but nymphs, they may have five dozen different patterns in their vests and know precisely which fly to use and how to fish it. What I am talking about are what I call "selective" fishermen who fish the same fly any time, anywhere without giving any thought to what would be the best tactic for a specific section of water.

The culmination of reading a stream comes after you have made your fly selection, where you want to fish the stream, and how you want to fish it on clues or information you have gathered by investigating repeatedly each change in the stream's characteristics. Just reading a stream once on each outing is like reading the same page of a book over and over, for each new stretch of water is different from the one you just fished, and the same stretch will be different on another day. With those changes in stream features come possible changes in trouts' feeding preferences.

The real essence of reading a trout stream is as simple or as complicated as continuously observing the stream and its environs for factors that may influence trout behavior. These factors would include stream features such as riffles, pools, and cascades and bottom characteristics such as gravel, live vegetation, silt, rubble, or large rocks and boulders. Each type of habitat would contribute to a different type of trout life-style, providing such things as security lies, feeding stations, rise forms, and even a selective food preference caused by some organism that was plentiful in that specific type of trout water.

Reading a stream is like learning to fly cast—all those drawings and detailed photos make it look simple, and it is not a difficult skill to acquire, but you learn to fly cast by fly casting. You learn to read a stream by reading streams—lots of them.

If you tend to do more wading and casting than you do detective work and catching fish, then you should begin to schedule some investigative work. For every one of those conspicuous mayflies you see floating on the surface like sailboats, there are thousands of other organisms beneath the surface, in the gravel, under rocks, flying in the air and climbing around on the stream banks.

Many fishermen suffer from a condition I call lazy eyes; being so absorbed with casting or seeing how fast they can fish one big pool and race (in the water, of course) to the next that they miss some obvious clues and some that are subtle. A wasp nest hanging over a stream may alert one angler only to beware of getting stung. However, an angler who has learned to stay in a perpetual stream-reading frame of mind will see the same wasp nest and realize right away that a realistic imitation of a wasp drifted downstream from that nest just might drift in front of a trout that had eaten wasps before.

Just using your eyes in a constant searching of wind, water, and stream banks will increase your awareness of the places trout live and the variety of things they like to eat. When you have started to really use your eyes, you have begun to look at the pictures in our hypothetical book, but there is still some information that is eluding you. You must dig for all the little tidbits of data you can collect, for the more data you process, the more accurate your assessment of the trout in that specific stretch of water.

You will have to get down on your knees with one of those nets that are used to catch tropical fish and scoop some burrowing nymphs out of the silt in the crevices in the stream bottom to get some models for fly size, silhouette, and color. Turn over some rocks and, using a nymph seine, catch samples of the nymphs that reside under it. Hold on to some of those flat rocks you turn over and take them to shore for closer scrutiny, for many of the clinging species of nymphs will not let go of their rock just because you happen to move it around a little. A wide-mouthed terrestrial net with a fine mesh will give you a good idea what the landlubbers look like. Don't limit the use of your terrestrial net to just those insects you see flying around or crawling. Sweep the net against foliage and blades of grass to pick up insects that are too small for you to be able to see.

Once when team teaching a session on reading a stream at a trout-

This angler is focusing his attention on the easily fished open water and missing some of the best water, which is in the boulder-strewn hard-to-fish section behind him. Photo courtesy Don Pfitzer.

fishing school we astounded the students with the variety of organisms we had collected out of the stream: sculpins, dace, crayfish,
salamanders, and many varieties of nymphs—crawling, clinging, burrowing, swimming, nest-building, and case-building. With our nymph
seines we collected carcasses of several specimens floating in the surface film. But we really blew the students' minds when several of us
began flailing the streamside foliage with big terrestrial nets. They
thought we were nuts, until we showed them the tremendous biomass
of terrestrial and aquatic insects that had been present on the vegetation overhanging the stream. One student said afterward that he had
been trout fishing for nearly fifteen years and never realized that so
many insects could be in the overhanging brush.

*A 35mm single-lens-reflex camera with a macro lens is a good tool
to record trout food specimens for future reference. The small
Plexiglas aquarium confines specimens to a small area to simplify
close-up photography.*

Insect field-guide books can provide detailed instructions on how to preserve insect collections if you want to keep specimens for future reference. Many serious students of entomology even keep nymphs in aquariums. Although it is difficult to keep nymphs out of fast-flowing water alive in a home aquarium for very long, they usually last long enough to make the results worth the effort.

Realistically, we should recognize that imitating the food organisms that trout feed on is not difficult; the tough part is finding out what they look like.

This terrestrial insect, floating in the surface film of a stream, was collected by holding a nymph seine in a major current flow for several minutes.

4

Don't get any closer to a stream than absolutely necessary to make your cast. Keep a low profile and use streamside vegetation whenever possible to break up your silhouette.

Presentation

PRESENTATION, AS I DEFINE IT, begins when you get up in the morning. That supposedly lucky hat or bright red shirt probably does bring you a lot of luck—all bad! It just doesn't make sense for a fisherman to select dozens of fly patterns that differ only subtly in color shades, to deceive a trout's highly color-sensitive vision, but then adorn himself with the brightest clothing he can find. A guerrilla fighter would by this logic camouflage his pocketknife and wear a flame-orange jumpsuit.

As much consideration should be given to what you put on your body as to what goes on your tippet. Clothing should be selected to match the background as closely as possible. Because it is usually impossible to select an outfit that will match all the backgrounds you might encounter in a day's fishing, you have to play the percentages and select clothing that will blend well with the most common background you expect to encounter during the course of a day's fishing.

I don't recall ever having fished any trout waters where my flame orange deer-hunting shirt would have allowed me to blend into the surrounding landscape, but I'm sure that just as I have you have encountered many fishermen clad as though they were bound for a deer hunter's convention. I can't state absolutely that you will never catch a trout while clad in a red shirt, but I contend that you will catch more and bigger trout if your quarry is not aware of your presence on the stream.

It is all too tempting to let enthusiasm cause errors in the early stages of presentation. It is very easy to allow sight of a rising fish or the discovery of what appears to be a prime lie or feeding station to generate tactical mistakes in approaching the fish. Before any water you expect to fish is ever approached, it must be thoroughly scouted and a sequential series of casts planned in advance. Only after you have determined the specific locations you want to cast to and exactly where you want to be positioned when you will make those casts can you then approach the casting position.

A sneaky trout fisherman will catch more trout than a fancy long distance caster who knows the Latin name of every insect on his side of the Continental Divide. Whenever possible, utilize streamside cover to conceal your presence. Finding this cover should be one of the decisive factors determining your casting position.

Casting from a kneeling position is a technique that should be in every fisherman's repertoire. About the easiest way I know of to spook a trout and send him undercover to a security lie is to show him your silhouette against the open sky. When a trout has you in a backlit position against an open sky, all your casting motions are visually amplified. If you cast from a kneeling position and use streamside cover, the chances of you or your casting motions being detected are much less likely. Any cover that will break up your silhouette should be used.

Your success will be directly proportionate to how low you keep your profile. The importance of a low profile and no silhouette increases as you get nearer to the fish or waters you suspect of holding fish.

If the knees are not the first part of your waders to wear out, you are not using streamside cover to its maximum potential or maintaining an absolutely low profile. It is impossible to accomplish these two objectives without spending more time on your knees than a full-time participant in a floating crap game.

It is a good idea to always approach trout from a downstream direction when you are moving into position to make a cast; since trout *usually* face upstream, you are less likely to be observed if you approach from directly behind. But care is always in order. For example, recently I was trying to get some trout pictures for a magazine article. My son Chris was to approach the pool from a downstream direction and try to catch a fish from what we suspected was a good patch of holding water. I snaked up to the edge of the bank on my belly and peered over into the pool—sure enough, there were half a dozen good fish holding in a section of water about four feet deep. After I got in position and had my cameras ready, I signaled Chris to ease upstream and fish the pool. He gave me a funny look when I told him to be extra careful, because most of those trout were facing downstream.

If you always assume that trout invariably face upstream, it will cost you some fish. Be aware of the possibility that trout may be facing downstream, especially in waters where deep pools have reduced current flow to practically zero. It isn't difficult at all for a trout to hold himself in a position facing downstream when the current flow is practically nonexistent. A swirl or eddy of current can often cause water actually to flow upstream for short distances. If such an eddy exists near a trout's feeding station or security lie, he could very likely be holding in a downstream-facing position. So don't assume that all trout will be facing away from you if you approach them from a downstream direction. I suspect that over 99 percent of all the fish you come in contact with *will* be facing upstream, but you still have to stage your approach assuming one may be looking your way.

Even if a trout is facing directly away from you as you maneuver into a casting position, you are not completely safe. Because of his exceptional peripheral vision a trout can see a full 330 degrees, leaving only about 30 degrees directly behind him as a blind spot. Even when everything is just right and you do approach a fish from directly behind, you don't have very much of an advantage, but take it any time you can get it.

Never be lulled into a false feeling of security that you are undetectable if you are approaching promising-looking water from a downstream direction. It is not as likely that your presence will be detected if you are downstream from a trout, but it is not an impossibility.

I prefer to wear chest-high waders, even in small, relatively shallow streams where hippers would seem adequate. Chest waders permit you to kneel down in waters that would come up over the hip boots that end about midway up your thighs.

Kneeling on stream banks or in streambeds can be rough on the knees of both wader and fisherman. To protect the knees of your waders you can glue over each knee a patch made of a section of truck-tire innertube. A set of kneepads like those worn by basketball players or wrestlers worn inside your waders can ease the discomfort of kneeling on a rock-strewn stream bottom.

Unnecessary and reckless wading are major contributors to unsuccessful trout fishing. If you consistently catch fewer and smaller fish than your associates, there can be several reasons, but the primary factor is probably injudicious wading.

Wading in a trout stream is like marriage; it shouldn't be entered into without a great deal of thought, and then very cautiously. Before hopping into a stream clear up to the suspender buttons on your waders, take the time to study thoroughly that portion of the stream. Look for possible security or feeding lies where trout may be holding near where you plan to enter the stream. If you suspect that a fish may be holding near your point of entry, fish that spot first from shore. This precautionary tactic has resulted in my catching many fish that would have been otherwise spooked and lost had I not fished an area of stream I was about to enter.

After you have decided you must enter the stream, do so with all the haste of preparing for an IRS audit. Good waders are so slow and cautious that they hardly appear to be moving at all. The only things hasty wading will do for you are to provide hilarious pratfalls to fill your fishing buddies with glee and save you a lot of time. The time you save will be that which is normally used in playing and releasing fish or cleaning a few to eat at the end of the day. Rapid wading will certainly allow you to fish a lot of water, but most of the fish will be gone before you get within casting range.

Wading can often be detrimental to success in small streams. Fish in a small stream have only two defenses when you nearly tromp on their giblets: they can panic and dash, either upstream or down. When this happens you don't lose the opportunity to catch just one but many fish, for that spooked fish takes off to avoid being trampled and darts past others, who are in turn put into full flight. In a small stream this chain reaction can be transmitted for a considerable distance. You don't have to nearly step on a fish to startle him into a fullblown panic—heavy footfalls or the clunk of dislodged grapefruit-sized stones can warn him of an ominous approach.

There are many natural sounds associated with the flowing water in a trout's world: a perpetual murmur as water flows over riffles, stones, and boulders; a nearby waterfall with a gentle roar; small stones clicking and clacking as the current shifts them. A trout lives with these subtle sounds all its life and will not become unduly alarmed by them.

A cautious wader rarely generates more than an infrequent gentle sound that can blend in with the normal stream-produced noises, but a wader who moves hastily and creates loud noises in a steady rhythm can alert trout well outside his effective fishing range. Comparing hasty and cautious wading techniques is very similar to comparing two deer hunters in the woods. One walks heavily in a steady, fast pace. A bedded deer hears the threatening approach and leaves the county. The slow stalker who generates only a few quiet, widely spaced sounds will be more apt to surprise that big old buck lying in his bed. The same philosophy is applicable to trout fishing in that you must sneak up on them while they are feeding; the only trout you will ever catch are the ones that are unaware of your presence.

It is easy to let enthusiasm overshadow your judgment and cause you to wade too fast or carelessly. Discipline yourself to move with caution and you will not only catch more fish but you will also spend a lot less time dragging yourself up out of the creek, emptying your waders and pouring the water out of your fly boxes.

If you keep a low profile and wade like a sneak thief, you will have a major part of presentation under control. Now you must apply yourself to getting a fly close enough for a trout to take it. Much has been written about the various merits of specific-length fly rods, but I believe too much emphasis has been placed on rods and not enough attention given to fly lines.

You can buy a seven-and-a-half-foot fly rod that will take any weight line from an 8 down to a 4, but I would hate to have to cast a size 10 hopper pattern in a strong wind with a 4-weight rod, no matter how long it was. Conversely, I wouldn't like to try to cast a skater pattern near a big brown in still water with an 8-weight forward-taper line and hope to perform the feat with any finesse.

Fly lines have come a long way in both function and design since the early piscatorial pioneers flung their flies on lines of braided horsehair. The modern angler has a cornucopia of line designs, colors, and space-age materials to choose from. A good selection of fly lines will add more versatility to your angling repertoire than a whole closetful of different length fly rods and a dozen fishing vests full of gadgets.

To simplify a complicated subject, the American Fishing Tackle Manufacturers Association has adopted a system of codes for identifying the various properties of fly lines which gives vital information on taper, weight, and density. The AFTMA Fly Line Standards for weight are based on the weight of the working part of the line—the first 30 feet—exclusive of the tip in the taper.

Code Number	Line Weight (in Grains)
# 1	60
# 2	80
# 3	100
# 4	120
# 5	140
# 6	160
# 7	185
# 8	210
# 9	240
#10	280
#11	330
#12	380

To differentiate between the various physical properties of various fly lines, the AFTMA has established the following codes:

L = level   F = floating
ST = single taper   S = sinking
WF = weight forward   I = intermediate,
DT = double taper   floating or sinking

Once you have learned the code you can immediately identify a line marked DT6F as being a Double Taper #6 (160 grains) Floating; WF8S as a Weight Forward #8 (210 grains) Sinking; L9F as a Level #9 (240 grains) Floating.

Most fly rods are marked by the manufacturer with a recommended line weight. As a general rule you can use a line that is one number higher or lower than the one indicated on the rod. For example, a rod marked #7 will probably cast a #6 and a #8 satisfactorily.

If you buy a reel with easily interchangeable spools, you can easily change from one type of fly line to another as fishing circumstances dictate. A few spare spools having various lines can add instant versatility on a stream. With this type of arrangement you can change from a floating double taper to a sinking tip about as quickly as you can change from a dry fly to a nymph.

Specific details on how to use the various fly lines are in the chapters which deal with the various categories of fly patterns, but I think some comment in order here on the characteristics of the various line designs.

The Double Taper (DT), Floating(F) is currently the most popular fly line and by far the biggest seller, since it is the most versatile of all fly lines for general trout fishing. As the name implies, this line has a double taper, one on each end of the line. If one end begins to show wear, just reverse it on the reel and you have for all practical purposes a new fly line. The gradual taper on this line allows a gentle presentation with dry flies and casts well over both short and medium distances. Since it floats, it is ideal for fishing dry flies on the surface and can be pressed into service for fishing nymphs below the surface in shallow water by adding a few tiny split shots at the barrel knots in your leader.

A Double Taper (DT), Sinking Tip (ST) would be a better choice for fishing nymphs, streamers, or wets in water that was over three or four feet deep and doesn't have any appreciable current flow.

A Double Taper (DT), Sinking (S) would be the best choice for fishing streamers, nymphs, or wets in deeper, fast-moving waters.

A Weight Forward (WF), Floating (F) is a favorite of mine for casting size 10 or 12 grasshopper patterns in late summer, especially on large streams. The added weight in the forward section of the line permits better accuracy with the bushy hopper patterns, in addition to greater distance with a minimum of false casting. It is also a good choice for those occasions when you are fishing dry flies on large streams or on windy days. As a general rule, I had rather make a short cast as opposed to a long one, but where streams are not conducive to easy wading, the WT is my choice for making those long casts.

A Weight Forward (WF), Sinking (S) is without equal for fishing streamers, wets, or nymphs in large, deep streams with strong currents.

I usually keep about six fly lines either in my vest or close at hand when I am fishing: three double tapers—one floating, one sinking tip, and one sinking; and three weight forwards—a floating, a sinking tip, and a sinking. This combination allows me to have a line perfectly suited for almost any situation I may encounter.

After you have perfected the skills of approaching to within casting distance of a trout without being detected, then you must make a cast that puts a fly into a trout's field of vision with such finesse that it looks like something good to eat, which is when casting skill is indispensable. You can learn to be a good caster as a by-product of doing a lot of trout fishing, but you will never reach your full potential as a fly caster if you don't spend a lot of time practicing your casting technique. If you find it impossible, as I do, to concentrate on catching a fish and perfecting casting technique simultaneously, you should practice casting so much that every motion, every subtlety of timing, becomes a natural reflex. This stage of perfection and casting finesse comes only with many hours of casting spent far away from trout waters.

Tennis players, golfers, and trapshooters all practice technique before they ever take on an opponent, and you can bet that the really good casters you have known spend many enjoyable hours with their favorite long fly rod when not on a stream. If you don't have access to a body of water to practice your casting, a large, grassy lawn will suffice. Casting on any surface except water will wear out a fly line, but two or three fly lines worn out on the back lawn will be the best investment you will ever make in becoming the best possible fly caster you can possibly be.

If you don't have easy access to trout waters, spend as many afternoons and weekends as you can flyfishing for panfish. You will not only keep your casting skills honed to a razor edge, you will also be keeping other skills sharp, such as setting hooks.

Your casting repertoire need not consist of a multitude of fancy showboat-type casts that look impressive when diagramed on the pages of a magazine or in some learned volume on trout fishing. If you discipline yourself to master completely a half dozen or so practical casts, then you will be way ahead of the average trout fisherman. You should be able to control the gap in your line loop as you cast, keep the loop closed tight when casting into the wind, and open it up when you have to make a long cast with the wind at your back. You should master the roll cast, an indispensable maneuver when fishing small streams in close quarters where a backcast is impossible. You need to be able to do a few "slack-line casts" for those times when you have to place a fly upstream from a fish and get a natural drift over his feeding station. A simple serpentine cast with your line having a lot of S curves in it when it falls on the water will suffice. A check cast will accomplish the same thing. A single- and double-haul cast is good to know for those occasions when some extra distance is required. Add to these a right- and left-curve cast and you should be able to put a fly just about any place you want it.

5/

Attractor patterns usually don't even resemble a natural insect, but their high visibility and ability to look like something a trout might like to eat make them very effective.

Attractor Patterns

ATTRACTOR PATTERNS come in several different types, including dry, streamer, and wet.

I have separated "attractor" patterns from "suggestive" patterns and devoted a chapter to each because I am convinced that trout take each type for a different reason. An "attractor" pattern, such as the Royal Wulff, does not resemble anything that occurs in natural form in a trout stream. A "suggestive" pattern, such as the Adams, actually resembles several types of natural trout food and could be mistaken for any one of several naturals that occur in a stream. Many fishermen may disagree with my categorization of some patterns, which is fine— differences of opinion are what make horse racing, politics, religion, and fishing.

Some of the attractors' characteristics are that they are highly visible, the dry versions are more buoyant than the conventional sparsely dressed drys, they are durable enough to withstand numerous chewings by trout, and they allow an angler to fish fast, rough waters that would be difficult if not impossible to fish with conventional imitator-type patterns.

Some waters, such as a stretch of fast, broken water over a riffle, are ideally suited for fishing dry attractor patterns. As mentioned previously, a feeding station usually has two physical characteristics that a trout needs: relatively slow-flowing water as a place of refuge, and a nearby strong flow that will bring in a supply of food.

Many riffles have a patch of smooth water varying from something the size of a newspaper page to a large "slick." A slick, or patch of smooth water surrounded by rough, broken water, occurs when some

obstacle to flowing water is present. The obstacle can be nothing more than a shallow depression in the streambed, a ledge, a submerged boulder, or just a flat section of bottom surrounded by stone rubble. Slicks provide feeding trout with varying degrees of refuge from flowing water and fulfill the first requirement, refuge, for a feeding station.

The second requirement, that of fast-flowing, food-rich currents, surrounds a slick in the broken waters flowing over a riffle. Consequently, a slick surrounded by a riffle constitutes an ideal feeding station—one that is often ignored by the casual angler.

A trout that collects its food in one of these slicks does not have the opportunity to scrutinize it as closely as one feeding in a long, gentle run or at the tail of a big pool. If it spends a lot of time looking at its food, it will be gone. You don't find many fish that will closely examine a fly and then refuse it when you are fishing a slick.

Many anglers never detect a slick in a riffle, and many "match-the-hatch, dry-fly" purists ignore them, because it is difficult to get a sparsely dressed, barely buoyant mayfly imitation to float through a slick. Even if you did get a good float with a size 18 Hendrickson, the trout would have a hard time spotting it. The trout wouldn't be the only participant in this little drama that would have trouble seeing a size 18 Hendrickson; if you have ever tried to float a tiny, sparsely dressed fly through rough, broken water, you know exactly how hard it is to tell where it was at all times.

A slick in a riffle is created by the extreme differences between the

Lee Wulff's series of flies originally tied for salmon fishing has proven effective on trout as well. These high-visibility attractor patterns are good choices when fishing rough, broken water.

rate of current flow and the surrounding riffle. The very conditions that create the slick also make it virtually impossible to get a long, natural drift with a dry fly. Unless the slick is a large one, it won't require a drift of any significant length.

The smaller slicks are the ones that most often go unnoticed and consequently unfished, even in streams that are subjected to intensive fishing pressure. A fisherman could concentrate on these small slicks only and for practical purposes be fishing virgin waters, even in a heavily fished stream.

Helen, Georgia, is a small resort community that attracts hordes of visitors all during the year. The Chattahoochee River flows right through the middle of town and gets a lot of fishing pressure. A large, shallow riffle on the north side of town just inside the city limits is less than knee deep. Back in the days when I was legitimately employed and didn't make my living as a hunting and fishing writer, I often passed through Helen, at lunch time or the end of the working day. My schedule didn't permit the time to walk in to my favorite streams back off the beaten path, but I did know I could always take a few quick trout by slipping into my waders and working a Royal Wulff through a few slicks right next to the highway.

This riffle was within easy casting distance of the town's largest restaurant, and my success rarely went unobserved by the several trout fishermen who always seemed to be in attendance there. After my first fish or two would come the inevitable question, "What are you catching them on?" They would always don their waders and move into the shallow riffle a polite distance away to begin casting, with little or no success.

Soon the dirty looks would begin to come my way as they began to suspect I had lied about what I was using. My imitators occasionally caught a few small trout feeding in the shallow riffle, but I always took more fish and larger ones, because I was fishing the Royal Wulff in several small slicks where the bigger fish were on feeding stations. Half the battle in fishing attractor patterns effectively is knowing where to fish them.

Because a slick is surrounded by a wide variety of current flows of different velocities, it is almost impossible to get a drift of any appreciable distance before the fly is pulled under by drag on the line. In small slicks this problem is of little consequence. Just make a slack line cast, such as an S curve or serpentine cast, that allows your fly to touch down just upstream of the slick in the very end of the broken water. The disturbed surface of the broken water will camouflage the landing of your fly, and it will be drifting naturally in the slick before the fish ever sees it. It is not necessary to cast a fly any appreciable distance above the slick to get a natural drift, since the trout won't be able to see the fly very well, if at all, until it leaves the broken water and floats into the slick. By eliminating unnecessary drift in the riffle above the slick, you reduce the required length of the drift.

When a fish is feeding on surface food that is floating through a slick, he must take it quickly or it will be lost in the broken water downstream from the slick. Because of this "catch 'em quick or lose 'em" routine, a trout feeding in a slick has very little time to count the caudal appendages on any fly pattern that drifts through his window. Success in fishing a slick is often determined by whether or not a trout sees your fly at all, rather than how closely it duplicates, say, a size 22 midge.

The trout-fishing literature is strewn with the claims of aspiring fly designers who proclaim the deadliness of their latest "original fly pattern," but it is not difficult to come up with a fly that is different and occasionally catches a fish. But Lee Wulff's fly patterns, such as the Royal Wulff, White Wulff, Blonde Wulff, Grizzly Wulff, and Grey

Wulff, have separated him from run-of-the-mill fly designers and put him in the rare handful of fly designers who have made an original, significant contribution to the fly-caster's arsenal.

Lee's hairwing flies have the high visibility, high floating style, and durability that make them deadly on many types of water. His flies are excellent producers on many types of water, but they are unmatched in rough, broken waters and the slicks found in them. I would as soon go fishing with only the butt section of my fly rod as be caught trying to fish rough water or slicks without any of Wulff's patterns. I realize that Lee designed some of his hairwing patterns to be mayfly imitations, and I apologize for adapting them as strictly attractor patterns when no hatch is occurring, but the end results justify the means.

In addition to an ample supply of Wulff patterns, try to include some other highly visible, extremely buoyant patterns in your vest, such as the Irresistible with its deer-hair body, the Rat-Faced Mc-Dougal, the Cooper Bug, Goofus Bug, Humpy, and Haystack. All these patterns are composed primarily of deer hair, which makes them float in rough waters where some of the more conventional styles would soon be submerged.

In spite of what some angling scribes would have you believe, trout are often opportunistic, not always selective feeders. In some streams that do not support massive and frequent aquatic insect hatches, a trout must feed in an opportunistic manner if he doesn't want to go hungry. Fish in these types of streams, and even those in streams that have major hatches but none in progress, must feed on a wide variety of different food forms. To see just how important opportunistic feeding is on some of the streams you fish frequently, keep a record of what percentage of the fish you dress have more than one type of food organism in their stomach contents over the span of an entire season—your concept of how frequently trout feed selectively may suffer a serious setback! I would never make a categorical statement about all the trout streams in this country that suggested that the ratio of opportunistic feeding was greater than that of selective feeding, but it is important to realize that opportunistic feeding does occur in every stream to some degree, and it is important to determine just how prevalent it is in the streams where you fish.

When fish are feeding opportunistically, they take a variety of food organisms that happen to drift into their field of vision. They are not particularly concerned about the exact appearance of a fly pattern. It is important that a fly look like something good to eat, but it is also important that the fly be highly visible.

As a general rule, when trout feed opportunistically it is because food in a given species is not predominantly available. Consequently, they feed randomly on a wide variety of food organisms. The high visibility of an attractor pattern is a definite asset during the times when trout are watching for anything that looks like food but are not particularly concerned about the exact silhouette, color, and size of the flies they take.

In addition to the patterns already mentioned, you may want to add some variants to your list of flies to try during a nonhatch opportunistic feeding period. Variants are not specific patterns but rather a style for tying various patterns. A variant is merely a fly that has been dressed with tail and hackle at least one size larger than would be used normally on a given-size hook. Most variants are not as sparsely dressed as usual. Therefore, a variant has a longer tail and hackle than a standard dressing and is dressed a little heavier to give it a somewhat bushy appearance. The result is a more highly visible, better floating fly that produces between hatches.

Art Flick was a major contributor back in the 1930s to the development and popularization of variants, with his patterns that can be described as being half body and half hackle. They were intended as mayfly imitations, but they also make excellent attractor patterns when no mayflies are present.

Some of the better variant patterns look like standard ones that have a thyroid problem. One experiment worth your time would be to tie up some variant versions of your favorite standard patterns that imitate the natural insects found in the streams you fish. It is not a complicated project; just tie some heavily dressed "magnum" patterns on the same size hook you normally use.

Like many fly patterns, the Irresistible has many color variations. Some of the more productive ones are the Adams, the White, the Black, the Yellow, and the Brown Irresistibles. The original version of this versatile pattern may have been tied to imitate a natural, but its reputation has been built on its high floating properties and visibility. An Irresistible will stay on top in all but a class-five rapids, and you can see it as well as the fish can.

The Cooper Bug is another pattern that consists primarily of deer hair and is a proven taker of trout. This pattern is an easy one to tie and rivals the Irresistible for durability.

The Humpy pattern, called a Goofus Bug in some parts of the country, is claimed by some fishermen to imitate a large stonefly or big caddis. In the smaller sizes, fishermen claim that it duplicates small caddis flies or even little mayflies. Another of the deer-hair flies, the Humpy has that property which makes it fall into my attractor category—high visibility.

The Hornberg was tied originally as a wet or streamer fly, but in recent years it has become popular as a highly visible dry fly. I am often amused to meet fishermen in different parts of the country who share their "secret weapon" fly with me, which turns out to be a dry Hornberg. The secret is out, now, from Alaska to the southern Appalachians.

On the surface is not the only way to fish attractor patterns. Wets can be deadly when tied in bright, highly visible colors. The Parmachene Belle was a standard with fly casters a few generations ago. I must confess that most of my success with this pattern has been in streams well off the beaten path—it really produced for me on several rainy afternoons fishing for cutthroats in Alaska's Wolverine River, where it accounted for as many trout as the two local streamer favorites, the Mickey Finn and the Silver Doctor.

Fishermen often comment that the Parmachene Belle works well only in remote, far northern streams where trout don't see many anglers or artificial flies. I believe that the success of this pattern in these waters is more due to the opportunistic feeding styles necessary for survival than to a lack of fishing pressure. Since selectivity is not a primary concern in these waters of sparse insect populations, the maximum visibility of wet patterns like the Parmachene Belle is a definite asset.

When an attractor pattern is called for, don't overlook the salmon flies. These gaudy, highly visible patterns are attractors in their purest form. Since salmon don't feed as they migrate upstream in their spawning runs, they strike the brilliantly hued flies for some other reason, depending on your own theories of why salmon strike when they are not hungry. I'll leave such theorizing to the piscatorial psychologists and just deal with what I know. Salmon flies don't look like natural insects and salmon aren't hungry anyhow, so what makes them strike? The only answers are high visibility and motion.

Trout will also succumb to flashy streamer patterns, especially in those far northern streams where insects and other food organisms have a tough time. During the times between hatches, when trout are feeding opportunistically, either by choice or necessity, they will also take flies that were tied primarily as salmon patterns.

Once I was attempting to catch salmon on Alaska's Wolverine River just upstream from where it flows into Yes Bay, using a bright pink pattern called the Polar Shrimp, which was deadly. This salmon fly was taking cutthroat trout on about one cast out of three. As I experimented with other multicolored salmon patterns, I had the same problem—the cutthroats wouldn't leave them alone.

When I got back to the lodge that evening and faced the inevitable question, "Did you catch any salmon?," I deviated from the angler's norm and told the truth: "Nope. I was fishing for cutthroat. Caught a whole bunch." I never did tell them it hadn't been a matter of choice.

While on a backpacking/trout-fishing trek in New Mexico's Sangre de Christo Mountains in the early seventies, I met a resident trout fisherman who was doing much better than I was. It was early July and as hot as the place where all worm fishermen go when they die. The local angler was using a pattern he called the Fore and Aft, consisting of hackle tied at the shoulder and the bend of the hook. He graciously gave me a few, which I wore out, or rather those high country New Mexico trout wore them out, and I wound up at home without a model for a pattern.

Flies of a fore-and-aft design come in several patterns, one of the better known patterns being the Renegade, which consists of white hackle up front, a brown hackle tied at the rear, and a peacock-herl body in between. Like all other patterns that catch a few fish, the fore-

and-aft design is subject to being "invented" regularly by someone who comes up with a new color combination and declares that he has created a new wonder fly. I have found fore-and-aft patterns to be producers in just about any combination of colors, as long as one of the hackles is a fairly light color such as white, cream, yellow, or gray. With at least one light hackle in the pattern, I can keep up with the fly much better in rough water or during periods of low light.

Bi-Visibles are another attractor pattern that many modern fly fishermen have forsaken for some of the new, highly publicized hatch matchers. This sad state of affairs is their loss: a Bi-Visible is hard to beat when you have a wary old brown holed up under an undercut bank next to a long, smooth run. Since the Bi-Visible is all hackle, it is a super floater when well dressed with dry-fly floatant. This combination of high visibility and superior floating properties makes it a prime choice for fishing long drifts on glass-smooth waters. The standard colors of a white hackle tied in front of a brown Palmer-hackled body is as productive as any colors I have used. You might find it useful, as I have, to tie up a few that are almost half white and half brown for use in poor light.

Since you are not attempting to imitate a natural insect when using attractor patterns, they have another advantage—they can be fished by methods that afford maximum visibility. As with streamers, wet attractor patterns are often at their best when allowed to drift downstream and stripped back up against the current. Usually I first work water very gently and cautiously with attractor patterns, then, if nothing happens, I impart bolder motions to the fly, until finally it fairly streaks back upstream. To many this may sound illogical, but how many times have you floated a fly perfectly over a feeding fish and gotten no response, just to have him smash it after it has sunk below the surface and you were reeling in to move on to more cooperative trout? If perfect drifts executed with finesse haven't produced, what have you got to lose by stripping a fly rapidly through the water before you move on? It doesn't work all, or even most of the time, but it does work frequently enough for me to continue to do it when nothing else has worked on a fish I know is feeding in a specific area.

6/

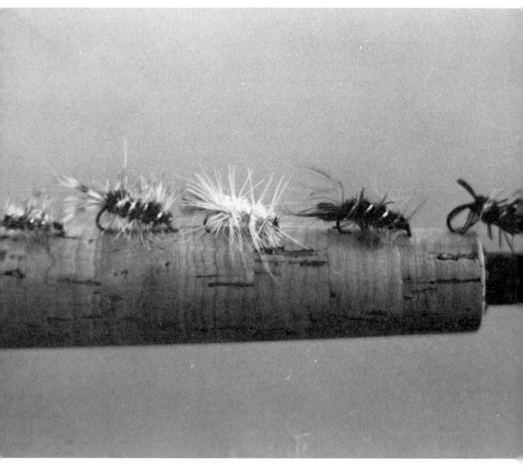

Wooly Worms are standards from east to west and are proven producers. These multiple-choice patterns don't duplicate any specific food organism exactly but are frequently taken by trout that may be feeding on anything from stonefly nymphs to caterpillars.

Multiple-Choice Fly Patterns

THE NUMBER-ONE-SELLING DRY FLY at Orvis for the last decade or so has been the Adams. A specific pattern does not maintain that degree of popularity on the strength of just a pretty face alone—it has to catch fish, and catch them on many different types of trout streams. If a national outdoor magazine were to survey its readership and ask the question, "Which aquatic insect does the Adams imitate?," the replies would probably include most of this country's mayflies plus several other species. Strangely enough, most, if not all, of these replies would probably be right, which accounts for the popularity of the Adams pattern. The Adams does resemble many insects closely enough to fool trout, even when they are feeding selectively. When trout are feeding opportunistically, the effectiveness of the Adams is compounded, because it suggests many different food organisms that may tempt a trout's palate.

Many devotees of the "match 'em exactly" fraternity look upon users of suggestive and attractor patterns as being just barely above the "worm washers" or "corn dunkers," but the only opinion that needs to concern us is that of the trout, which looks with favor upon suggestive patterns.

Those who adhere to the exact imitation philosophy will argue at length about whether a pattern should be tied, say, with caudal appendages made of two strands of chipmunk whisker or the scrotum fuzz of an albino pocket gopher. Whenever I am exposed to these learned discussions, I listen politely then ask a simple question that has yet to get a logical answer: "How do you account for the presence of the largest, most prominent single appendage on those immaculately constructed flies designed to imitate exactly a specific insect—the bend and point of the hook?" I have yet to see an insect that has a steel appendage protruding from its abdomen. Size, silhouette, and color must be the only factors that deceive trout into believing that an artificial is in reality an edible insect.

There are many ingenious fly patterns that are suggestive of several insects and offer trout a multiple choice. Using a multiple-choice pattern is like having several flies in the water at the same time; since it resembles several insects, a trout can believe it to be any one of the bunch.

H. G. "Tap" Tappley, long an advocate of multiple-choice fly patterns, popularized his appropriately named Nearenuf fly pattern in the early 1960s. Tap's recipe for the Nearenuf calls for a tail, of two striped grizzly quills; the body, to be a peacock quill; wings, made of a wood duck flank feather; and hackle, of mixed ginger and grizzly. Tap ties the pattern in sizes 12 to 18 but favors sizes 14 and 16.

The Nearenuf was the solution to Tap's desire to design a fly that resembled several of the mayflies common on many of the trout streams in his part of the country. Happily, the Nearenuf has also resembled many of the mayflies on most of the streams the rest of us fish.

Tap contends that the Nearenuf imitates the Quill Gordon, the Red Quill, the Hendrickson, the March Brown, the Grey Fox, and the Light Cahill closely enough to fool a trout, and I concur. Obviously, the Nearenuf doesn't duplicate any of these patterns exactly, but it does accomplish what Tap set out to do—it resembles all of them. A selection of this pattern in a variety of sizes would be good insurance, especially when you are fishing a stream for the first time and don't know what to expect trout to be feeding on.

I don't know if Tap played a role in the development of another multiple-choice pattern he made famous in his *Field & Stream* column, the Cooper Bug. (Let us pause for a moment while all the hatch-matching purists gnash their teeth over a trout fly with *bug* in its name.) To build this fly, start off with fly-tying threads attached at each end of the hook shank, then wind on a body of peacock herl. Lay a bunch of deer hair on top of the hook shank with the tapered ends toward the bend of the hook. Tie in the butts of the deer hair tightly right behind the hook eye. Next tie the deer hair down tightly at the bend of the hook. The hair will flare out at both places where it was tied. Trim the hair off short behind the eye of the hook. I have seen versions of the Cooper Bug tied with many different colors of deer hair and have tried a few myself, but natural deer hair seems to work about as well as anything.

In addition to its resembling several different forms of trout food, the Cooper Bug is so effective when fished in the different ways it can be that it's hard to fish in a manner that won't produce a few fish. When it is dry and dressed with a little dry-fly floatant, it is an excellent surface fly, even in fast, broken water. As it becomes water-logged, it can be fished just below the surface. By adding some leader sink, it can be fished as a wet, nymph, or streamer pattern. I have even clipped off the flared deer-hair tail and used it successfully as a beetle pattern after trout had chewed up my supply of those patterns and beetles were what the trout were interested in.

The Humpy, discussed in the last chapter, also bears mention as a multiple-choice type. It does resemble several thick-bodied ter-restrials, but I'm sure that in addition to this appeal it has made many trout take an impromptu trip to the frying pan because they thought this multiple-choice fly pattern was a still-born nymph that hadn't succeeded in making the transition from a nymph through the nymphal shuck into an adult.

The Haystack also deserves mention as a multiple-choice pattern. Although the hatch-matching specialists don't have much trouble with the name of this fly, they shudder at its bushy wings and "bass bug" appearance. This pattern, originally from the Northeast, was designed primarily to afford a bold wing silhouette for use in rough waters. It has since been modified in various sizes and colors to imitate mayflies, which it does copy several species of—simul-taneously. One of the current, highly touted mayfly-matching gurus has admitted in print that one of his wonder flies is an adaptation of the old standard Haystack. His patterns do imitate mayflies—and a lot of other food organisms—at the same time!

Another fly pattern that is recognized by all, carried by many, but fished by few is the old standard Royal Coachman. Modern anglers use this fly as a last resort, because they can't find a mayfly in any of the current literature that looks exactly like it. Unfortunately, too many modern fly fishermen wrongly assume that a fly is no good unless it looks so much like a mayfly that the naturals buzz around the fly box with propagation of the species in mind. The Coachman has survived because it resembles several species of both aquatic and terrestrial insects.

Rare indeed is the fisherman who didn't have a Royal Coachman in his first box of flies. The Coachman produced in the beginnings of our angling careers in spite of the fact that in those days we cast with the finesse of a three-hundred-pound one-legged ballerina, waded like an aquatic snowplow, and thought a feeding station was a hamburger joint. With so many things going against us, we still caught fish on the Coachman because it looked like several different types of trout goodies, without matching any specific one exactly.

The term *searcher pattern* is synonymous with *suggestive pattern* or a multiple-choice pattern because it is generally used when there are no obvious signs of feeding fish. When confronted with this situation, most fishermen logically use a technique known as fishing the water or searching for fish. This practice is considered by many to be comparable to shooting ducks on the water, which I frown on. But when I am on a stream with a fly rod and there are no obvious—or even some inobvious—clues, I'll begin to go through my fly box.

One of the first steps I take when I don't know what to do first is to tie on one of the multiple-choice patterns, such as an Adams, Nearenuf, Cooper Bug, Humpy, Royal Coachman, Royal Wulff, or one of the other Wulff patterns. I go fishless sometimes (but like every other fisherman, I lie about how often), but more often than not that unhappy circumstance is avoided by using all the multiple-choice flies in my vest before resigning myself to defeat.

I rarely cast randomly to various parts of a stream. Some thought goes into where possible feeding stations, prime lies, or security lies may be located and then into planning my casts and drifts accordingly. Trout fishing is a combination of art, science, skill, determination, luck, and a lot of guessing. If I am fishing the water, I reduce some of the guesswork by using multiple-choice patterns, which allows me to concentrate primarily on where the trout are and to allow the suggestive pattern (which resembles several food organisms) to offer a trout several possible choices of just what type of groceries my fly looks like. After I catch that first one, a stomach pump or autopsy will give more specific clues as to what food sources are present and which the trout are eating.

If regulations allow it, a small seine will be of great help in identifying just what is in the stream for trout to eat (see Chapter 3). Invariably, the contents of your seine will reveal the presence of many varied food organisms. The net will allow you to reduce the number of possibilities of just what the trout are eating, but rarely will it give you a specific answer about what they are feeding on. After seining for food items on the bottom, in the current runs, and on the surface, sort the lot by size, shape, and color. After you have divided your catch into several piles of insects that are similar in appearance, select a multiple-choice pattern that most nearly duplicates the largest pile, then if that doesn't produce, select a pattern that duplicates the next largest pile. I admit this may be unscientific, but it works frequently enough to make the exercise worthwhile.

Another pattern that has become a standard in many fly boxes in one of its numerous variations is the Muddler Minnow. This is another of the patterns that would get a wide variety of answers if a cross-section of anglers was queried about which food organism it imitated. Some possible answers might be sculpin, stonefly, or even grasshopper. All could be correct, depending on how the Muddler was fished.

When tied as a weighted pattern with a few turns of fuse wire applied to the hook shank and doused with leader sink, the Muddler can be twitched along the bottom on sink-tip fly line in a performance suggestive of a sculpin doing whatever it is that sculpins do on a stream bottom. When tied on a light wire hook and dressed with some dry-fly floatant, it could pass for a large western stonefly, even if the trout you were trying to catch wasn't myopic. A high-floating Muddler could also be worked near a grassy shoreline to suggest a grasshopper out for a late summer swim.

Another pattern I consider to be a multiple-choice pattern is the popular Wooly Worm. This pattern is a standard with the oldtimers who have fished Yellowstone Park for longer than most of us have been out of three-cornered pants. Wooly Worms two or three inches in length are not uncommon on western streams like the Madison. The most often accepted story about this fly's origin is that it was developed as a nymph imitation for the salmon fly, or "mighty big stonefly," to eastern fly fishermen. That may be true, but ask some fisherman who adheres to this theory of its effectiveness to let you compare it with a replica of a caterpillar from his fly box. I rest my case.

I don't deny that a Wooly Worm looks like a salmon fly nymph, but I believe it also looks like a lot of other trout food. My fly box has Wooly Worms in black, yellow, two shades of green and brown, and I have caught fish on all four patterns. But there ain't no such varmint as a nymph that comes in all those four colors and ranges in size from a long-shank size 12 to a three-inch monster. However, they look like something good to eat, and as long as trout keep taking them, I'll keep fishing them and could not care less what a trout thinks when he takes one.

You may have noticed how rare an ugly girl is after you have been in the bush for a month. When a trout is feeding opportunistically, he probably has a similar low threshold of acceptability, so a pattern that offers several possible interpretations will probably take fish.

The coast-to-coast popularity and effectiveness of the Wooly Worm is probably due to its ability to look like several different trout food organisms.

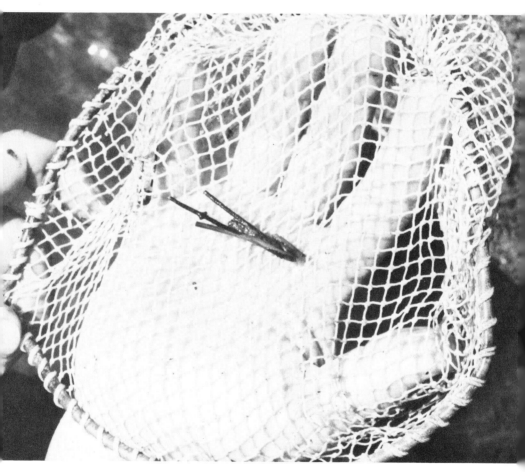

The well-camouflaged case of a caddis fly. A nymph collector who is
not on his toes might discard the case as debris.

Fishing the Nymph

SOMEONE COULD FISH just nymphs every day of the trout season and probably catch more fish than if he used any other combination of fly patterns. Research biologists say that trout food consists of 60 to 85 percent subsurface forms. The highly touted aquatic hatches may last for only an hour or so, whereas the nymph form of that same insect may exist in that form for as long as three years.

Nymphs are available to trout on a year-round basis, so fish feed on them primarily in an opportunistic manner. Nymphs come in a wide variety of forms, some models that swim and some that don't. Some angling writers have made a career out of thinking up intricate maneuvers for fishing nymphs "correctly," but the more I fish nymphs, the more suspicious I am of those piscatorial theoreticians who deal in absolutes.

Even the most casual worm drifter needs to know only two things about how to fish nymphs: drift the nymph just as you would a worm, and set the hook any time you detect a telltale line movement. I have met several fishermen who are deadly nymph practitioners and all they use are ultralight spinning tackle and split shot.

The same ingredients for success are applicable to fishing nymphs with a fly rod; just drift the nymph deep, and set the hook up on each suspicious line movement. Before going into detail on the first step, let's cover the second.

Several years ago I was doing a story on a man who was a legend because of his success at catching bass on the plastic worm. We were not in the boat very long before I began to notice how frequently he set the hook on such submerged objects as stumps, roots, and tree tops. As the afternoon wore on I couldn't resist needling him a little about how often he set the hook on inanimate objects. "For a guy who is supposed to be a crackerjack worm fisherman, you sure have a lot of trouble telling the difference between a strike and a stump." His answer was one of the most valuable fishing lessons I've ever had. "You are right, I do have trouble detecting the difference between a very gentle pickup and bumping some underwater obstacle. Rather than not set the hook on a gentle strike and miss a fish, I just set the hook every time I feel something on the end of the line. I hang a lot of stumps, but I also catch a lot of fish. If I set the hook and it isn't a gentle strike, I haven't lost anything. If I get a subtle strike and don't set the hook because I think it is a stump, then I have lost a fish." That is not only good advice for plastic worm fishermen, it is also applicable to fly fishermen using nymphs.

A few years after that enlightening experience I had an opportunity to see this "set the hook on anything suspicious" theory tested under scientific conditions. At the annual meeting of the Outdoor Writers Association of America, Paul Johnson of the Berkley line company had set up an experiment by stationing some scuba divers in a lake. We were instructed to cast a plastic worm toward the diver's bubbles and then work the worm back to shore in the same way we normally fished a plastic worm. The divers were equipped with a device used to capture tropical fish, a small hand-operated vacuum pump that could ingest the plastic worm just as a bass would suck it into his mouth.

We were instructed not to set the hook but to count the number of times the worm was "picked up." Less than half those pickups were detected by the forty-two writers who participated in the test! I would not suggest that outdoor writers are the best fishermen in the world, but we are probably not the worst either. The point is that if a largemouth bass can inhale a six-inch plastic worm with such finesse, then imagine how subtle and undetectable would be the gentle ingestion of a nymph by a trout as it drifted by his nose.

Any change in fly-line posture, no matter how subtle, should trigger a hook set. If the line drift slows down, set the hook; if it speeds up, do the same. A tap or twitch, no matter how slight, should be responded to with a hook set. If your nymph has bumped some underwater obstruction or been influenced by a subsurface current and you set the hook to find no fish on it, you have lost nothing. You have merely added a lifelike twitch to the nymph, which can then be allowed to drift on its way. If you did get a subtle strike that you thought too gentle to be a trout and ignored it, you have lost a fish. Ask yourself how many times you have seen a trout take a fly on the surface and not felt any appreciable signal at your fingertips. The biggest majority of trout caught on nymphs have probably not been detected by the angler until the fish has already hooked himself and bolted for cover. It also seems likely that most of the nymph pickups go undetected by the casual fly fisherman who waits for an arm-jarring jolt before setting the hook. A healthy dose of suspicion and a quick trigger finger are the two greatest assets of a successful nymph fisherman.

To fish nymphs most effectively you need to get them down close to the bottom, if not right on the bottom. In large streams that are relatively free of large obstructions, many fish will hold right on the bottom to take advantage of the relatively slow-moving current that flows right against the bottom. In some streams this "bottom cushion" is the only refuge they have from flowing water. Large areas of obstacle-free stream bottom tend to scatter trout, and nymphs can be drifted over these long stretches more efficiently than can a fly on the surface.

There are several methods for getting a nymph down deep quickly and keeping it there. Obviously, a sinking-tip line is a real asset, as are weighted flies and a few tiny split shot attached at the blood knots of the leader. If you are fishing a stream bottom that is saturated with tiny crevices which are constantly snagging the split shot at your leader knots, you may want to attach a few lightly crimped shot to a short dropper on your leader rather than at the blood knots. If the shot on the dropper get snagged, a gentle pull will strip them off without breaking off a part of your leader.

On the subject of droppers, don't overlook the advantage of attaching a second nymph on a leader dropper. Fishing two nymphs at once may not double your chances for a strike, but it can certainly improve the odds. If you haven't found a specific pattern that is working well, experiment with various sizes and patterns. A dark nymph combined with a light one of a different size is a good way to fish when you haven't been able to detect trouts' preference for a specific pattern. To add further versatility to a tandem rig, put a weighted nymph on the dropper and an unweighted pattern on the tippet. Then you will have one right on the bottom and the other slightly off the bottom.

The dilemma of which pattern to use can frequently be resolved with the use of a small nymph seine to determine which species are most prevalent in a particular stretch of stream. The availability of particular nymph types can change as frequently as the types of stream bottom change. The nymphs present in fast water flowing over shallow riffles would be rather scarce in water flowing slowly over a bottom with debris such as leaves or sand.

Just as few anglers have any real concept of the enormous biomass that exists as immature aquatic insect forms in a trout stream, so do they rarely appreciate the infinite variety of nymphs present in a stream, a variety conducive to frequent opportunistic feeding patterns. There are times when trout will feed selectively on one specific type of nymph, as when they are taking emergers just prior to or during a hatch, but usually they are quite willing to take any nymph that exposes itself.

Fishing a nymph directly upstream is a demanding and often frustrating endeavor, but sometimes it is the only way to take larger fish in a heavily fished stream. They view with suspicion any fly that deviates appreciably from the normal velocity of drifting natural insects. This is a fine point that borders not on splitting hairs but on quartering them. Admittedly this technique is one that I use only when I know I am working a larger and warier than average fish.

If trout are aggressively taking nymphs, especially when they are in competition with one or more other fish, then the across and upstream cast will do the job. Under these conditions you may even take fish by stripping in line after the nymph has drifted directly downstream from your position. It is not what you would call a common occurrence for a trout to take a nymph that is being stripped directly upstream against the current, but neither is it rare; it happens frequently enough for me to continue the practice.

Most fishermen fish nymphs across and upstream. This method is the most conducive to detecting strikes by touch, since the current flow rapidly takes excess slack out of the line. Casting directly upstream and stripping in slack line as the nymph drifts toward you requires a little more finesse and maximum attention to detecting strikes, but it is the best method for simulating and duplicating exactly the drift velocity of natural insects, since your line doesn't have a big cross-stream bow in it (as with the across and upstream cast) to add velocity to the fly's drift.

Several lines can greatly improve your nymphing success, depending upon the type of water you are fishing. A light-colored floating line is a good choice for fishing nymphs in fairly shallow water that isn't too rough. The high visibility of light-colored lines, such as ivory or salmon, greatly improves your ability to detect subtle indications of a strike. Some fishermen like to use a brightly colored marker of some sort at the junction of the fly line and the leader butt.

In water that is too deep or too fast to fish a floating line, a sinking tip is a good choice. For the deepest and fastest waters, you may want to go to a high-density sinking line. When using such lines, the best way to detect a strike is by the sense of touch rather than trying to detect visible line movement. Remember that no matter what type of line you use or which method of detecting strikes (sight or feel) you prefer, set the hook upon any suspicious line behavior.

As a general rule, the greatest populations and variety of nymphs will be present in shallow riffles. Because riffles are the favorite lair of most nymph varieties, it is understandable that trout like to collect in the deeper waters just downstream from riffles. Any water just downstream from a riffle that looks like it might provide a place for trout to hold is as good a place as you will ever find to fish nymphs.

One of the best nymph fishermen I have ever shared a stream with is Don Pfitzer, a native Tennesseean who has spent many years pulling trout out of streams all over this country with a technique he calls "the Tennessee Drift." I first observed this deadly nymph-fishing method of Don's when he and I were fishing on the Little Tennessee River, before this river's excellent trout fishing and last remaining snail-darter habitat was destroyed.

Don casts his fly well upstream from a trout's suspected feeding station, then allows the nymph to sink and drift in the current near the bottom. If the trout doesn't succumb to this presentation, Don raises his rod tip slowly and simultaneously strips in line in two- or three-inch segments. This gives the nymph the appearance of struggling toward the surface to split its nymphal shuck and hatch into an adult. It's a rare trout that can resist this performance.

As a general rule, nymphs are usually my first choice when I confront a situation where there are no obvious signs as to what trout may be feeding on. A little work with a nymph seine and looking for clinging-type nymphs on the bottom of rocks from the stream will usually give me a few clues as to which nymph patterns to use.

Different species of aquatic insects prefer different types of water. A net-building caddis fly will be found in a different type of water than a caddis that builds a case out of debris and small twigs. It is a good policy to change nymph patterns as stream configurations change. Immature forms of aquatic insects are highly specialized organisms, which should be kept in mind when selecting nymph patterns.

Nymphs pursue a wide variety of life-styles as clingers, crawlers, swimmers, and burrowers. The clingers are generally broad and flat and are found in fairly fast to swift water where the bottom has large rubble and stones. Crawlers and swimmers are usually fusiform (fish-shaped) and can be found actively moving around in moderately swift water. Burrowers are for the most part located in slow-moving waters where silt has collected, which provides them with a medium to burrow in. This oversimplification of the various nymph types can be used as a guide for selecting general patterns.

There has been a trend recently among nymph fishermen to lean toward the "fuzzy" type of nymph patterns, with emphasis on size, shape, and colors that resemble either clingers, crawlers, swimmers, or burrowers rather than trying to duplicate exactly one specific species of nymph. Many nymphs have external feathery looking gills similar in appearance to the fuzzy-bodied patterns, which are suggestive patterns that appear to be a live organism resembling several different types of nymphs.

A small net with a stiff wire rim is ideal for collecting burrowing nymphs from stream bottoms consisting of sand or sediment.

Any of your favorite fur-bodied nymphs can be tied in the fuzzy style by spinning the fur loosely when tying them or using a needle to pick out hair fibers after they are tied. The longer strands of fur protruding from the fly body give a realistic impression of the natural nymph's external gills working in the current. This is especially desirable when working an imitation of a swimming nymph in fairly slow-moving water.

Nymph fishing can be as simple or as complicated as you want to make it. An angler can go into detailed entomological research and know the Latin names of every nymph in his section of the country, if this is what he enjoys doing. But he doesn't need a master's degree in entomology to be a deadly practitioner of the art of nymph fishing— as long as he learns what basic types of nymphs are present by using his nymph seine and remembers that nymph forms change as stream conditions change.

8 /

*A fine-meshed nymph seine is a good way to collect nymph specimens
from a stream. Hold the net close to the rocks you are disturbing—if
you hold it too far downstream, the nymphs will get back under cover
before they can be swept far enough to be caught.*

Fishing
the Prehatch

BECAUSE AQUATIC INSECTS may exist in nymphal form for a year or more, their survival depends upon their ability to keep a low profile and elude detection by hungry trout. The various species utilize several methods of doing so, including hiding under rocks or in gravel and weeds, burrowing in silt and sand, adopting camouflage coloration, and even covering themselves with a protective case, maneuvers that make it fairly difficult for feeding trout to detect them.

Most aquatic insects are most vulnerable during their nymphal phase, just prior to emergence as an adult. Immediately before this transformation, they must leave the security of stream-bottom cover and make their way to the surface by swimming or floating or by crawling out on the bank. Their vulnerability during this prehatch stage often triggers vigorous feeding activity by trout. With the exception of those insects that must spend some time riding on the surface aboard their nymphal shuck to dry their wings prior to flight, most nymphs are now at the most vulnerable and most visible period in their lives.

Caddis flies have a complete life-cycle, consisting of the egg, larva, pupa, and adult stages. Case-making varieties of caddis flies just seal off the end of their case as pupation begins; the free-swimming varieties form a pupal shell somewhat like a cocoon. At the end of the pupation period, the pupa bursts out of its case and rides to the surface with an assist from gas bubbles it collected prior to erupting from its case. Theoretically, this is supposed to be a rather rapid ascent, which it is in the majority of cases or the species wouldn't survive. Sometimes, however, the mission aborts or is partially aborted, providing easy prey for trout. Even when everything goes well, the emerging caddis pupa is vulnerable to consumption.

When an emerging caddis reaches the surface, he doesn't dally, but immediately spreads his wings and flies off. Many fishermen see the caddis flying off the surface, see surface disturbances caused by trout feeding on pupa beneath the surface, and wrongly assume that the trout are taking adults off the surface. Many anglers even have trouble detecting a caddis hatch, because of the caddises' practice of springing right off the water as soon as they reach the surface. Laboring under this erroneous assumption, they drift dry caddis fly after dry caddis fly over feeding fish, with unhappy results.

Another thing that often makes a caddis hatch hard to detect is that most of them are spread out over longer periods of time than hatches of many of the other aquatic insects. About the best indication that a caddis hatch has occurred is the presence of adult caddises flying mothlike just over the surface of the stream. The presence of adult caddises over the water may indicate that a hatch is occurring, just occurred, or happened even several days ago. Unlike most mayflies, whose entire adult life-span may range from only twenty-four up to seventy-two hours, caddis adults may survive for over a week.

Because the emergence of the adult caddis from the surface is so difficult to observe, and caddis hatches may be less concentrated than those of other aquatic hatches, and adults may be present over the stream for over a week after they hatch, how do you determine when to fish a caddis emerger pattern? If adult caddises are present above the water, it can be assumed that there has been a recent hatch or one is currently in progress, so even if trout are not actively feeding on emergers at the moment, they may be receptive to an emerger pattern, since they will have fed on caddis emergers in the recent past.

The presence of the adult caddis flying just above the surface is so obvious that it is understandable why most fishermen often capture a specimen and duplicate it with a dry fly. This is a sound angling tactic that will produce fish on occasion. If you have never tried it, try a caddis emerger next time you observe adults over a stream—you may find that you catch somewhat larger fish.

A good indicator that trout are feeding on emerging caddis flies is the presence of bulges, gentle boils, or rings on the surface without the presence of bubbles. Usually a trout that is taking surface food will ingest small amounts of air that are then expelled through the gill openings and appear on the surface as bubbles.

If caddis flies are making their trip to the surface from water that is several feet deep, the surface bulges and boils may not be present, since the trout will be catching them well below the surface. The observant angler can detect this deeper feeding on emergers by the telltale metallic flashes created by light bouncing off the sides of feeding fish.

To simulate emerger behavior, you must get your fly down onto or very near the bottom, which can be best accomplished with a sinking-tip or sinking-fly line. Since you want to get the fly onto the bottom as soon as possible, use emerger fly patterns tied on heavy hooks, with perhaps a few turns of lead wire applied before the fly is dressed. In fast water you may even elect to add a few shot at the blood knots of your leader. An additional fly attached with a dropper can increase your success when fishing emerger patterns.

If depth and current speed permit, you can fish directly down-stream by letting your fly settle to the bottom and then drifting it to a section of stream you suspect contains fish that are feeding on emergers. When you think the fly is within visual range of a feeding fish you can initiate one of several different performances to imitate emerger behavior.

If you are using a caddis emerger pattern, your fly should make a fairly rapid ascent to the surface. This can be achieved by having your rod parallel and close to the surface as your fly drifts along the bottom. When the fly reaches a prime location, lift the rod and raise the tip. This will cause the fly to rise to the surface at the same no-nonsense pace used by the caddis emergers.

If this rapid rise doesn't produce a strike, then repeat the rod movement but pause several times as you lift the rod. This will cause the fly to pause and drift downstream slightly before continuing its journey to the surface. As an additional emerger technique, lift your fly off the bottom with the rod tip, then drop the tip back to the surface. This will cause the fly to rise up off the bottom and begin to settle back toward the bottom. Be alert for a strike as the fly is settling back. It seems a mistake for authors of trout-fishing books to speculate about what goes on in a trout's head, but it is a temptation few can resist, and I am no exception. I believe that trout take a descending emerger pattern fished in this manner because they think a chunk of good eating is about to return to the safety of stream-bottom cover, so they grab it on the way down to avoid this unhappy circumstance.

Frequently, water depth and strong currents prevent the direct downstream emerger tactics just described. In these situations you will have to cast across and upstream to allow sufficient drifting time for the fly to reach the bottom, where all effective emerger maneuvers must begin. It requires some finesse to coordinate the arrival of your fly on the bottom in the area you want to fish with the beginning of its ascent. It is often difficult to know exactly where your fly is at all times during this extended across-stream type of fishing. I don't be-lieve any fly caster can know exactly where his fly is when it is bumping along the bottom in a fast current, no matter how expert he claims to be. The only way to know for sure that you have covered a promising patch of water is to fish a series of emerger maneuvers with each one a little further downstream than the previous try. It is good practice never to assume that you have executed an emerger performance in front of the desired audience, even when you are fairly sure of your fly's exact location. Saturate the vicinity with several encores.

All emergers don't have the caddis fly's ability to perform its quick trip to the surface and rapid takeoff. Some of the mayflies make a much slower trip to the surface which involves a good bit of drifting with the current. These mayflies are best imitated with a sink tip or floating line and a nymph that is not quite as heavily weighted as one for caddis. Since the slow-rising emergers spend an appreciable amount of time traveling horizontally, it is not as critical for flies imitating them to begin their performance on the bottom of the stream. A drifting fly can be animated and given the appearance of one of the weak-swimming nymphs or a nymph having problems leaving his shuck. An occasional stripping in of about six to eight inches of line as the emerger pattern drifts in the current will often take fish during a prehatch when one worked in a dead-natural drift won't.

Sometimes an emerger pattern merely has to be suggestive of an emerging nymph. Trout usually feed selectively on emerging nymphs, so some realistic imitation is required. One of the best ways to determine which emerger trout are taking and what you need to imitate it is to use a nymph seine. Mine is made of fine-mesh window screen wire that is attached to two wooden dowels. When I suspect that emergers are on the menu, I place the net in a run and leave it for several minutes, which can seem like an eternity when fish are feeding. Be careful not to disturb the bottom upstream from your seine position, because if you stir up nymphs in the gravel or rubble they will get caught in your seine and make it appear that some species dislodged from the bottom was in the process of making its way to the surface to shed its nymphal shuck—which it wasn't. To draw a representative sampling of the emergers you need to imitate, you must have your net in a substantial flow of water and must hold it in place long enough. How long is long enough is difficult to say, since this varies with the intensity of the hatch and the volume of water flowing through your net.

Once you have some naturals, duplicate them as closely as possible in size, shape, and color. After selecting the closest imitation in your fly box, determine the most realistic method of fishing it. If the nymph is one you recognize and are familiar with, you will have a pretty good idea of the ritual it performs in making the transition from a water-dwelling nymph to an airborne adult. It is a good idea to save a few specimens you are not familiar with to take home for identification. Being able to identify some of the common aquatic species in streams you fish frequently is not only conducive to future success but is almost as fascinating as the actual fishing. Ernest Schwiebert's *Nymphs, A Complete Guide to Naturals and Their Imitations* is an excellent reference for the angler who wants to identify nymph specimens and also contains valuable information on the behavior of nymphs and fly-tying techniques for duplicating them.

On the topic of fly fishing for trout you can get in a lot of trouble. I do not mean to imply that emergers and stillborns will always outfish drys every time on every stream, but I am convinced that it is worthwhile to try both versions when trout are feeding on the surface and emergers and stillborns are in the water. The prehatch (and, in the case of the stillborns, the "almost hatch") are well worth any efforts you make to imitate them. Stomach samples of fish taken during a rise indicate a decided preference for nymphs and emergers over duns, sometimes as much as four or five to one. This preference could very well be because the immature forms are easier to catch than an adult with flight capabilities.

There are emerger patterns for most of the more common aquatic insects, but it is possible that you may not have a duplicate of a specific emerger for which trout are showing a decided preference. If so, a standard unweighted nymph can be fished on the surface by applying some dry-fly dressing. It won't float up high on the surface film like a dry fly, but then it doesn't need to if it is to simulate an emerger attempting to wrestle free of its nymphal case in the film. I have improvised emerger patterns by clipping the wings and some of the hackle fibers off of adult dry-fly patterns.

Emerger patterns fished in the surface film or just under the surface an inch or two will often take more fish than will working one all the way up from the bottom of the stream.

It requires no small amount of self-discipline to refrain from using a standard dry-fly adult imitation when a hatch is in progress, if you aren't getting any fish. The natural reaction for the angler who sees trout rising all around him is to keep changing his patterns in hopes of discovering some "masked," "concealed," "camouflaged," or "compound" hatch matcher that will produce success.

In recent years floating nymphs have gotten a lot of press. To some fishermen this concept of fishing with a nymph pattern that floats is an aberration that borders on piscatorial perversion. At first glance a floating nymph may seem like a bastardization of two respectable forms of fly fishing, nymphs and drys, but the concept actually has sound biological rationale to support it.

Several aquatic insects appear on the surface still enclosed in a nymph case, which splits open only after they reach the surface. This case floats on the surface film and the emerging adult climbs out and perches there to dry out his wings enough to allow him to fly. This exercise takes anywhere from around a minute to several minutes. In any case, it requires that the emerging nymph spend an appreciable amount of time on the surface breaking out of, crawling out of, or riding on his nymphal shuck.

While these emergers are involved in this insect version of a Houdini stunt they are vulnerable to feeding trout. Even if the process goes according to schedule, there is a period when they are easy prey. Frequently, the transition from nymph to adult meets with complications delaying the process, and sometimes it doesn't come off at all, resulting in a stillborn nymph, which is just about the easiest food a trout will ever consume.

The existence of stillborns and nymphs in the process of shedding their cases is all the justification needed for fishing nymph patterns as drys, either on or in the surface film. Even if you think trout are taking adults on the surface, it would be smart to try either emerger or stillborn patterns as drys prior to using a winged adult pattern. Several studies have shown that trout prefer the stillborns and emergers to adults.

More often than not, concentrating on the prehatch will produce more and bigger fish. Abandoning the use of conventional dry flies during a hatch is tough to do in the beginning, but after you have tried it a few times with some success it will grow progressively easier. Nothing builds confidence in a technique like success.

9/

Ant patterns are one of the better choices for fishing the nonhatch from late spring until frost.

Ant Patterns

VERY FEW trout fishermen's fly boxes—from Carolina to Colorado, from New Mexico to New England—would not contain several ant patterns, if a representative survey could be taken. A similar survey during mid- to late summer would probably also indicate that the popularity of this insect is widespread among trout also.

Of the several hundred thousand kinds of insects in this country, few are as widespread and numerous as the ant, which comes in no less than three thousand models and lives in colonies that may contain several thousand individuals. A bee colony may send out a swarm once or twice a year, whereas an ant colony may launch a dozen or so mating flights consisting of both males and females. As is the case with many other insects, male ants don't live long past their nuptial flight, and they often end up in the water looking very much like a spent mayfly.

Dead male ants don't have to fall directly into the water for trout to have access to them. They may expire on streamside vegetation or fall to the ground, to be washed into a stream by the next summer shower. Or a gust of wind often blows a flight of ants into a stream or surface of a lake. Conditions are particularly conducive to this mishap along streams and lakes at the higher elevations, where winds can be quick, unpredictable, and strong.

Sudden showers and the resulting ground-water runoff frequently float worker ants (which are wingless) into streams, where they become trout fodder. Wingless ants also can become victims of the wind when a sudden gust surprises them over the water on streamside vegetation. I suspect that this latter incident is not too common since an ant is very strong and it would take a rather healthy wind to dislodge one that was really clamped on.

Ants are probably more susceptible to being washed into a stream than most anglers realize. Their colonies are usually located on sloping, well-drained ground to avoid standing water that would drain into their colony's underground network of tunnels. This sloping ground adds velocity to the runoff water, which increases the chances of workers being caught outside the colony and being washed away.

Ants are not only plentiful and widely distributed but are active during almost the entire trout season. They can be observed during a warm day during the winter if the ground isn't frozen or snow covered. Even though ants are available to trout during the early parts of the season in some sections of the country, they increase in importance as the season lengthens and reach their annual population peak during mid- to late summer.

While preparing material for this chapter, I conducted a simple experiment to either prove or disprove one of my pet ant-fishing theories about how the naturals behave in the water. I was of the opinion that ant patterns, size 16 and smaller, worked best when fished on the top in the surface film and larger sizes worked best when fished just below the surface and deeper. After collecting a wide variety of ants ranging from sizes that compared to a size 20 fly down to some monsters that approached a size 8 and placing them in a small, wide-mouthed jar, some consistent patterns emerge.

The most obvious phenomenon was that the smaller the ants, the higher they rode on the surface film. The better they swam, the longer they avoided drowning and the longer they stayed on the surface after they succumbed. The large carpenter ants floated with the greater part of their body mass below the surface film from the moment they hit the water. The smallest sizes were quite religious and literally walked on the water for long periods of time.

Even the tiny ants that floated in the surface film considerably distorted the surface film. The higher an ant floated, the more obvious the surface distortion and the resulting refracted light became. Small fur-bodied ant patterns with a sparse hackle tied around the waist made a very realistic imitation of the way a natural ant looks on the surface.

Another revelation from my experiment would never have been noticed just observing ants in a stream. Ants have tiny hairs all over their bodies that collect minute air bubbles, which produce an iridescent sheen. This gloss can be arrived at by constructing ant bodies of spun fur or peacock herl. In the past I put a few drops of lacquer or fly-head cement on ant bodies to improve their durability, but after I observed the tiny trapped air bubbles on the bodies of real ants I brought that practice to a screeching halt.

As the ants increased in size, they floated less efficiently and consequently died quicker. Even after they drowned, the larger sizes continued to float in the surface film with about two-thirds of their body mass below the surface. This bit of information generated a new philosophy in my approach to the larger ant patterns. Previously I had used the larger sizes (12s, 10s, 8s, and 6s) as strictly subsurface models with heavily lacquered bodies and very sparse hackle consisting of only a few fibers on each side to suggest legs. I have since tied some dry ant patterns up to size 8, which have been most effective. I have not abandoned the hackleless lacquered ants in the bigger hook sizes, for they still take a lot of subsurface feeding trout; I just added some larger sizes that float in the surface film.

On opening day of the 1979 trout season, I was fishing the small Appalachian stream that flows about a quarter-mile from this typewriter and did well using a small size 18 fur-bodied black ant. This small stream is not noted for massive aquatic hatches, and as a general rule terrestrial, attractor, or suggestive patterns are better choices. I brought a few of my ant-caught trout home to cook on my smoker and, as we always do when a mess of fish are in the sink, the family gathered around for the "grand opening" to see what they had been feeding on. (When you live at the end of a one-lane dirt road in the Georgia mountains, you take your entertainment wherever you can find it.) I was surprised to discover that every one of the trout was chock full of midges. I didn't recall seeing any midges while I was on the stream, but this may have been partly due to the fact that on opening day I am like a blind dog in a meat house—adrenaline and enthusiasm run so high that I am rarely the observant, calculating, objective angler I try to become as the season wears on.

Part of the imitation ant's magic may be its resemblance to several other trout food organisms such as (in this case) midges. Conversely, the opposite could be true: I wonder how many hatch matchers thought they were fishing midge patterns when the trout thought they were being caught on ants?

Another terrestrial that finds its way into many streams in swarms is the termite. I am surprised that some creative fly designer hasn't come up with a hotshot termite imitation. Winged-ant patterns are about as close to a termite copy as you can get. There are some differences between winged ants and termites, but they are not so obvious that they would require two separate fly designs. So maybe termites are another lookalike that ant patterns duplicate closely enough to fool a fish or two.

I have always expected ants to be an effective pattern on eastern streams, but I was surprised on my first trips out west to learn that they were also deadly on high alpine lakes in the Rockies. I once took a brief respite from an elk hunt to try for some cutthroats in a lake near Platoro, Colorado. My guide told me that there were cutthroats in the nearby reservoir, and he was right. They demonstrated a de-cided preference for fur-bodied black ants.

On a backpacking trip in northern New Mexico, I took a noon break near a small alpine lake and after a quick lunch decided to try for a few trout as an alternative to the dehydrated food I had been living on for the past week. By chance I had stopped for lunch on the upwind side of the lake. The breeze was not very strong and just steady enough to create tiny ripples on the lake. These were just enough to make it hard to spot the rising fish, which were taking something off the surface.

Since most of the fish seemed to be working on the downwind side of the lake, I walked around there before I began casting. After trying several patterns in an attempt to match some flying insects I wasn't familiar with, I put on an ant, which is one of those patterns I go to when I fail to guess correctly the object of selectively feeding trouts' attention. I'd like to be able to elaborate on some complicated sci-entific procedure whereby I deduced that those trout were taking ants, but the truth is that I hit on the pattern as a matter of pure luck.

Autopsies on the first two fish I caught revealed that they were feeding on ants that apparently were being blown into the lake. The wind was pushing them to the downwind side, where they were collecting in sufficient numbers to trigger a selective feeding pattern. To test this hypothesis, I continued to fish the ant pattern, which was a black fur-bodied style about size 18, around the lake. I took a few fish on the upwind side, but they were scattered and small, and none of the other patterns I tried produced. The ant on the downwind side produced so well in that small lake that what had been intended to be a brief stop for a quick lunch turned into a fullblown afternoon's fishing.

I have seen this same feeding pattern repeated on several other alpine lakes since I accidentally stumbled on that ant "hatch" long ago. I now take a pack rod on all my fall hunting trips out west and find it hard to resist flicking a few ants into any alpine lakes I come across.

Any time you collect a few winged ants in your nymph seine and no other organism is present in sufficient quantity to indicate which pattern would be a good choice, try the ant. If even one winged ant is present in a sampling, there is a good chance that a mating flight has occurred upstream and some other members of that flight have also terminated their aerial honeymoon in the drink. These "swarms," or mating flights, are rather dense, and the chances of just one insect or two ending in the water at a time are pretty remote. Even though a trout may not have locked into a selective feeding pattern, it may have taken a few of the remainder of the swarm in an opportunistic manner and be responsive to an imitation of those it has already eaten.

Ants are a good pattern for mid-day when nothing much seems to be going on and there are no apparent feeding patterns. Because ants are most active during the warmth of mid-day and their heightened activity often contributes to accidents that result in ants being where trout can get to them. These little disasters won't happen in sufficient quantity to trigger selective feeding, but they look tempting to a trout that has dined on several ants drifting in the current.

A sudden summer cloudburst will often trigger a feeding spree with trout feeding opportunistically on terrestrials. Some of the best fishing

I have experienced with ant patterns has come right after a shower when the water is barely stained. A heavy, extensive period of rain will usually put too much silt in the water; trout do not usually feed actively during periods of excessive turbidity. Even hatchery trout exhibit a reduced feeding behavior when turbid water comes into rearing ponds. One explanation I have heard is that the silt irritates their gills, causing them to go off their feed.

There seems to be a fine line where a little bit of surface-water runoff, which stimulates feeding, becomes excessively turbid and turns off feeding fish. In streams where the watershed has not been vandalized by unrestricted harvesting of timber or road building or the construction of another shopping center, turbidity may not be a problem, but, unfortunately, this type of stream is steadily disappearing.

It would take about four pack mules to carry them and six clerks to file your flies if you attempted to duplicate the three-thousand-odd ant species that crawl around this country. Chances are that several hundred of these different variations are present in the state where you live and fish. I have a manageable selection of ant patterns that have served me well in many different parts of the country in a variety of trout waters. In the wingless versions I carry black and cinnamon flies with fur bodies in sizes 12 through 18; in winged patterns, also with fur bodies, in sizes 12 through 18 I like black, red, and cinnamon patterns; and I still tote large, black lacquered patterns in sizes 6 through 14.

There may be some local varieties you are aware of that are not represented in this selection. Selective feeding on a specific ant does occur, but on most occasions any ant pattern that is close to what is in the water or on the ground around the stream will get results.

The ubiquitous ant is a staple food organism of trout from the Rockies to the Appalachians. Ant fly patterns in several sizes and colors should be in every fisherman's vest. Such patterns should also spend a lot of time on your tippet during the warm days of mid- to late summer.

10/

Crayfish are eaten by trout whenever they can catch them, so a crayfish fly pattern is a fine nonhatch choice.

Crustaceans

CRUSTACEANS have never been very popular with fishermen or fishing writers as models for fly patterns or models for fly-fishing techniques. Occasionally you will run across a few paragraphs on the subject or they will be mentioned in passing in some piscatorial dissertation devoted to how someone matched a size 28 midge hatch that was concealed by a simultaneous compound hatch of four dozen other "varmints." Scuds, sowbugs, fairy shrimp, and crayfish get very little exposure in angling literature, but one or several of these invertebrates are to be found in almost all trout waters. Their lack of popularity with fly fishermen could be due to the fact that they are not insects and also that they do not "hatch" as winged adults. This indifference to crustaceans is not shared by trout, which will feed upon them with gusto whenever the opportunity presents itself.

Scuds, fairy shrimp, and sowbugs are present in nearly all types of trout water where aquatic weeds exist. They feed and hide in this weedy cover, which accounts for their rarely showing up in a nymph seine placed downstream from overturned rocks. To capture representative samples of weed-dwelling crustaceans you will have to seek them in the foliage.

These creatures are very active and can be difficult to capture. Don't try to seine large areas at one time. Stick a nymph seine down into the weeds and stir it around in the vegetation immediately in front of the net. A thoroughly inspected handful of weeds will probably produce enough organisms for a representative sampling to determine size, silhouette, and color. Any plucking of aquatic vegetation should be done judiciously so as not to damage or destroy habitat and may not even be legal on some streams.

Streams are not the only trout waters where crustaceans are to be found. Some of the western lakes have phenomenal populations, one of the most noteworthy being Henry's Lake in Idaho.

In addition to being favored fare for trout, the crustacean patterns' effectiveness is increased by the fact that it is not one of those patterns that is fished to death. It's impossible to prove that trout retain memories of unpleasant experiences associated with some of the more common fly patterns, but I have observed that real "killer" fly patterns and bass lures tend to lose some of their effectiveness shortly after becoming the current craze with the fishing fraternity.

The most widely spread and most populous of the scuds is the genus *Hyalella*. Though smaller than most other varieties, only about one-fourth inch, this tannish gray crustacean is by far the most tolerant of water conditions and can be found in both freestone and limestone waters.

Sowbugs (also called cress bugs) are common in most limestone streams that have an abundance of their favorite cover, watercress, hence their designation cress bug. Another crustacean common in the eastern limestone streams is the yellow scud.

Trout feeding in flowing water tend to wait for the current to bring food to them, but when they feed in lakes they cruise in search of food. Since crustaceans serve as major food sources in so many weedy lakes, it is important to understand how to fish these waters.

Until I took a backpacking/trout-fishing trip in New Mexico's Sangre de Christo Mountains in the late sixties, all my trout fishing had been done in moving water. At that time in my fishing career I didn't know what a crustacean was or that they even existed.

About halfway through my ten-day walk, I came down out of the higher elevations and set up camp next to a small lake that was two acres in size at the most. Some previous camper had built a small raft and obligingly left it for the next fisherman to use. My enthusiasm was not even dampened by the weathered note attached to the raft, "Hope whoever uses this raft next has better luck than I did." I did consider for a moment that maybe there were no trout in the lake, since I didn't see any fish rising and a quick scout around the shore didn't reveal any trout cruising above the weed-covered bottom.

I took off my pack, postponed camp chores until after more important business could be attended to, and assembled my pack rod. The raft didn't have a paddle, but it did have a pole. After you got about fifteen feet from shore it was too deep to pole, so I had to paddle with the pole, which didn't make for rapid travel.

As the evening wore on, rising fish still didn't appear. Undaunted, I continued to cast dries in hopes of enticing a strike. Eventually I spotted a few fish cruising just over the tops of the weed beds. Aha: I thought; they are nymphing.

I tied on a Light Cahill nymph and a long leader with a split shot attached so I could get the nymph down where the trout were (at that time I had not discovered the wonders of sinking fly lines). I fished the water, making no attempt to cast to a specific fish. Because my nymphing tactics worked, I was convinced that I had correctly read the water and deciphered what the fish were feeding on, but my self-confidence was shattered after I cleaned the two trout I had kept for supper and checked their stomach contents. They were full of some weird-looking nymphs I had never seen before, which I later learned were not nymphs at all but scuds. My Light Cahill nymph was close enough in size and color to resemble scuds, and slowly stripping the nymph just above the weeds simulated their activity closely enough for me to fool some fish.

Now my tackle is a little more sophisticated. I have some crustacean fly patterns (the better ones of which look remarkably like the Light Cahill nymph), and rather than fish the water at random I try to cast well ahead of a cruising fish to coordinate his arrival with the passing of my phony crustacean. I am no longer surprised to discover crustaceans in the stomach of a trout that came out of a weed-filled lake.

With weighted fly patterns and sinking fly lines, you can use a countdown technique to determine when your fly is about to touch the weeds. Just before making contact with the tops of the weeds, begin a slow stripping retrieve of about four inches at a time, or a hand-twist retrieve to move the fly along just above the weeds. This method can be worked in just about any depth of still water. If visibility permits, you can coordinate the arrival of your fly with that of a cruising trout. Frequently, the water and light conditions won't permit you to cast to individual fish, so on these occasions you will have to cast randomly in whatever area you expect fish to be.

When you must fish the water rather than cast to a specific feeding fish, concentrate your efforts to waters that are four feet deep or less. The plants that attract crustaceans require sunlight and are therefore usually densest in relatively shallow water. These plants can grow at greater depths and may have some crustaceans and trout in deeper water, but generally you can expect to do better in shallower waters.

In flowing water, crustacean patterns will do best when they are fished either just above or right next to weed beds. Trout will often lie right in the weeds and use them for cover just as do the crustaceans they are feeding on. A trout will take up a feeding station by lying so that his body is covered by weeds, but just barely, so that he can see out to watch the water flowing over his head for dislodged crustaceans.

Trout will also lie in weeds and watch a run that flows close by for dislodged crustaceans. Others will set up on a feeding station in a run that flows next to weeds and take any cress bugs or scud that get caught outside the protective cover of the weeds.

Obviously, it makes sense to fish crustacean patterns in those sections of stream where trout are likely to feed on the naturals. Deciding exactly where to place your fly will take some stream-reading savvy, since it may be difficult to observe a fish hiding in watercress that darts up out of the weeds for a short spurt, then drops back down onto station in the cover without ever breaking the surface. The presence of a fish feeding in such a pattern can sometimes be detected by observing the dull metallic flashes that indicate a fish feeding well below the surface.

I have heard of trout rooting around in weeds to dislodge cress bugs, scud, and freshwater shrimp, not unlike the way a bonefish nuzzles the flats for food. I have never personally observed this procedure, but I have heard it from enough fishermen whom I respect to accept it. I would not hesitate to try to put a crustacean pattern in view of a trout that I saw working through a patch of watercress.

Many of the patterns that imitate freshwater shrimp, scud, and

cress bugs are tied on severely curved hooks. Some meticulous ob-
servers of trout food organisms have noted that when these organisms
are in the water they are relatively straight in posture.

One outdoor scribe I admire for his no-nonsense, practical approach to fly fishing is Ted Trueblood, who originated the Otter
Shrimp after a 1950 fishing trip to Henry's Lake, Henry's Fork of the
Snake, Wood River, Magic Reservoir, and Silver Creek. All these
waters are loaded with freshwater shrimp and scud, which Ted knew
were there, because he could see them darting around over the weeds.
Ted noticed that these crustaceans were straight when they swam—
not in a curved configuration, as most of the patterns that imitated
them. He tied his Otter Shrimp on a Mustad 7948A hook in sizes
6, 8, 10, and 12 with a body of dubbed fur mix from pale otter belly
fur and a little white seal. The throat hackle and tail are partridge.
This pattern looks a great deal like some of the cream-colored fur-
bodied nymph patterns, such as the Light Cahill I used in that New
Mexico lake long ago. How many trout feeding on crustaceans near
weed beds must have been caught by fishermen who thought they
were imitating aquatic nymphs?

Many experienced scud imitators prefer long leaders and only
slightly weighted flies when fishing moving water. When only slightly
weighted and fished in moving water, the fly doesn't sink too deep,
which would frequently snag in vegetation. Crustacean patterns such
as cress bugs, scud, and shrimp are deadliest when worked in open
water just above or alongside aquatic vegetation such as watercress,
millefoil, or algae beds.

Scud are capable swimmers, and patterns imitating them are most
realistic when fished with some added motion rather than with a dead
drift, whereas sowbugs or cress bugs are weak swimmers at best and
should be drifted in the current for maximum realism.

With the exception of the Rocky Mountains, where only one species occurs in a few streams, crayfish are common in nearly all our
trout waters. I have observed anglers on several occasions looking at
crayfish in their nymph seines to the tune of something like, "I'm
trying to collect some nymphs or other trout food samples but all I
keep catching are these damn crayfish!" Sometimes premature con-
clusions interfere with objective research. I know of no better ex-

ample than the angler who discards all the crayfish out of his nymph seine so he can get down to business and see what trout foods are present in a body of water.

We have heard and read so much about how important mayflies, caddis flies, stoneflies, and midges are and how they must be exactly duplicated during a hatch that we tend to neglect the obvious variations in opportunistic feeding patterns. It's a rare mess of trout that won't have several crayfish discovered during autopsies. The only clue that trout have been eating crayfish may be fragments of a leg or the shell-like carapace that covers the thorax. Sometimes the casual angler who takes the time to survey stomach contents will pass off fragments of crayfish anatomy as assorted beetle or other large insect parts.

Crayfish prefer to reside on stream bottoms that offer an abundance of cover, which may be in the form of vegetation, rocks, or soft sediment suitable for burrowing. Protective cover is more important for their survival than is food, because they are omnivorous and will eat just about anything that doesn't eat them first.

These crustaceans are predominantly nocturnal. I have supplemented more than one streamside campsite menu by pegging the head or entrails of a cleaned fish to the bottom of a stream with a small wooden stake and returning later to pluck the larger crayfish for hors d'oeuvres. Just plop the live crawdads into salted boiling water and leave them until they turn lobster red, then fish them out and peel and eat them—scrumptious! This little extracurricular activity will not only provide some tasty grub but will also impress upon you the dense populations of crayfish that are present in most trout streams.

I have listened to heated conversations among fly fishermen who are practitioners of crayfish fly fishing over the virtues of various crayfish pattern color schemes. Since it isn't rare to capture specimens of several different shades in the same stream, or even in the same dip of the nymph seine, I don't think specific colors are that important, but I do believe size, silhouette, and technique are conducive to maximum effectiveness when fishing these patterns. According to the *Scientific Anglers' Fly Fishing Handbook*, research shows that fish prefer small crayfish, with females preferred over males. Immature crayfish and females are small, less aggressive, and have a smaller pincer size than mature males. Trout don't enjoy getting grabbed by a set of big claws any more than you do.

Before I learned about this preference for smaller-sized crayfish, I soaked patterns of all sizes, including some monsters over two and a half inches long, laboring under the assumption that big fish must eat big groceries sometimes. To test this theory, I compared the results from small patterns with a reduced claw size with those of the bigger, more ferocious styles. I don't use anything over two inches long now, with most patterns being between an inch and one and a half inches in length. I also keep the claw size small on the ones I tie and trim back the ones that I buy or ones tied by friends, leaving just enough claw to maintain a crayfish silhouette.

Many crayfish patterns are tied backward on the hook, which is logical, since crayfish swim backward in short spurts. This design is ideal for retrieving a crayfish in quick strips. A crayfish spends a lot of time just crawling leisurely along the bottom—creeping forward. Thus, for maximum realism you need a few patterns tied backward and a few tied frontward. The latter get a heavy dose of lead wire on the hook shank prior to dressing the fly, to get it right down on the bottom where the crayfish does all his crawling. These patterns are retrieved slowly. The ones tied backward don't have weight built in but may have some added to get the desired depth. The extra weight is achieved by putting split shot on the leader (how much being determined by water depth and current speed), which will cause the fly to resemble a crayfish swimming just above the bottom. Of the two techniques, the crawling-type retrieve produces the most often, but there are times when the frantic darting motions of a swimming crayfish seem to be most effective.

Crayfish patterns have produced fish for me at all times of the day, but most of the larger fish taken on these patterns have come late in the day, early in the morning, or when I was fishing at night. I have taken some very nice fish after fishing the evening rise when most other fishermen had left the stream at that magic time when the crayfish and big trout begin their peak activity periods.

Many types of minnows can be collected in your nymph seines, to serve as indications of which streamer patterns to use.

Streamers
and Bucktails

THE ACCURACY OF THE OLD ANGLING AXIOM that big fish eat little fish is reinforced many times during a season when I examine the stomach contents of trout, but to be totally accurate it should read, "big fish and medium-sized fish eat little fish." Chubs, sculpins, dace, trout fry, horny-head suckers, and sticklebacks occupy the catacombs of trout with such frequency that I don't understand why streamers and bucktails are not used more regularly by trout fishermen.

Any self-respecting fly fisherman has at least one box of streamer patterns tucked into his fly vest and on occasion will catch a nice fish on a streamer. The fisherman is rare, however, who uses a streamer on his first cast or exclusively at specific times of the year, on stretches of stream that are conducive to streamer effectiveness, or before he has even tried everything else in his vest without success.

For much of my early fly-fishing career, the streamer was just one of those patterns I carried in my vest because it was expected of me. But as streamers turned more and more fishless days into productive ones and demonstrated their ability to tempt larger than average trout, they became first-string starters more regularly and less of a last-minute substitution.

The key to fishing streamers successfully is to make them behave in a lifelike manner. There are few absolutes in fishing, and you may take a few fish on streamers that are merely drifted along in the current like a nymph, but to achieve the streamer's most deadly effectiveness you must convert it into a living thing with enticing moves, darts, and twitches.

Streamers are at their best when fished right next to the bottom. In shallow waters no more than three feet deep, I like a floating line with a sinking tip and except under unusual circumstances rarely use a leader over five feet long. A shorter leader helps keep the fly down on the bottom where I want it. On occasion I will even add some tiny split shot to the leader next to the barrel knots, which helps keep the fly down next to the bottom in swift water. Most of my streamer patterns are tied weighted with fine lead wire wrapped around the hook shank. A heavily weighted fly isn't always necessary, but more times than not it needs the extra weight to keep the streamer right on the bottom so it will simulate a small minnow seeking food or cover.

On one of my early "bring 'em back alive" expeditions to collect various specimens of trout food for observation and study in my home aquariums, I captured a pair of sculpins in a small seine. Both specimens fared well in their artificial habitat and taught me many valuable lessons about how to fish streamers that imitated their species.

I placed the two sculpins into a ten-gallon tank just over an arm's length from my desk. For several days I could hear a faint rattling sound over the hum of my electric typewriter, but upon looking up at the tank I could observe no motion or explanation for the sound. These sounds would occur several times during the course of a day. The mystery was finally solved once when I was stumped with a syntax problem. I had turned the typewriter off and was staring blankly at the aquarium. The sculpins were both motionless on the bottom of the tank, which was how they spent 99 percent of their time, when one of them decided it was time to change position. He flushed like a small aquatic quail, did an underwater sprint for a few inches, and settled quickly to the bottom, where he resumed an absolutely immobile posture. The tank's bottom was covered with a layer of gravel about the size of number-two shot, and the propwash (tail-fin wash?) from the sculpin's sprint had washed the gravel against the side of the aquarium.

The sculpins used camouflage as a protective device, moving in quick darts, then immediately dropping to the bottom, where they remained frozen. Being able to observe this maneuver has made a significant contribution to my success with those streamer patterns that imitate sculpins.

Sculpins are widely distributed and present in many trout streams, which accounts for the success of streamer patterns representing them.

All my sculpin patterns are tied as weighted models and are allowed to settle directly on the bottom of the stream. I retrieve them in short twitches of eight to ten inches, then let the pattern settle immediately to the bottom. This is a difficult maneuver in fast water, but it is fairly easy to do in the slack waters of a large, deep pool or in eddies adjacent to sizable obstructions such as boulders.

Casting a heavily weighted fly can be a frustrating experience the first time. I was introduced to the technique one cold spring day on Vermont's Battenkill River near Manchester. I was attending the Orvis Fly Fishing School, during which my instructor had just netted a twenty-inch brown while demonstrating how to fish a weighted Marabou Muddler. When I fished that same stream a few days later, I made sure I was well supplied with the heavyweight Muddlers.

At that early time in my career I was using a 7-weight, double-taper floating fly line, and my attempts to cast that chunk of a fly were the source of considerable amusement for my associates. It looked like (and I felt like) I had never had a fly rod in my hands. The moral is to get yourself some weighted streamers, cut the hook off at the bend, and get some experience casting this abomination before you expect to cast it with any precision on your favorite trout stream. A weight-forward fly line will contribute considerably to your early mastery of casting a heavily weighted streamer.

Weighted streamers of the type just mentioned are deadly fare during the early season when waters are high and turbid with spring runoffs from snow melt and spring showers. At this particular time of the year the streamer should be your first choice—not a final effort when everything else in your vest has failed to produce.

Streamers can be fished in a wide variety of techniques. Often they are most effective in fast-flowing, broken water where it would be difficult if not impossible to fish more conventional patterns. Such swift waters will add numerous twitches and jerks to a streamer, contributing significantly to its lifelike motions.

A streamer can be cast upstream at a 45-degree angle and allowed to drift down in the current. Keep your rod low and parallel to the surface to eliminate as much slack line as possible. When slack line between the rod tip and fly is kept to a minimum, you can add lifelike twitches by stripping in short lengths of line through the fingers of the hand holding the rod grip.

As the streamer drifts past you on its way downstream, be alert for gentle taps or any subtle changes in drifting speed, which are frequently the only indication you will get that a trout has succumbed to the temptation of your offering. Whenever you are fishing a fly you cannot see, such as a nymph, a wet, or a streamer, set the hook at every suspicious nudge, line twitch, change in direction or speed of drift. If a trout sees your fly drift by, he may very well move off his feeding station and drift along with it in the current. If he is moving downstream with the fly and gently engulfs it, you won't get the obvious arm-jarring jolt that many fishermen require before they strike.

Many of the gentle nudges you feel or observe in your fly line will be caused by the fly or line's coming in contact with a stone or other underwater obstruction, or may even be a gentle twitch caused by moving water. If you set the hook and have not had a strike, you have only added one more lifelike motion to your fly's performance. If, however, you ignore a gentle strike and pass it off as a bump against a rock, you have lost a fish. I suspect that the biggest majority of the fish that are caught on flies fished underwater are detected by the angler only after the fish has hooked himself and dashed for cover.

As your fly completes its downstream drift, it can be retrieved upstream by stripping in line, either in short lengths of four or five inches, or a foot or two at a time. As a general rule, I start off with retrieves in short segments, and if several such retrieves don't produce, I work the same water, using retrieves in longer increments.

Another general rule of thumb is that when using imitator patterns (as opposed to brightly colored attractor patterns), I attempt to make the imitators appear to be natural baitfish moving in short spurts as they dart from place to place seeking food or cover. The brightly colored, gaudy patterns seem to be most effective when worked in a bold, fast-moving, highly visible fashion.

If I suspect that a patch of water holds one or more good fish, I generally start off with an imitator pattern and try to make it appear to be a small fish working around on the bottom. Then I try to make it look like an "injured minnow" struggling to make its way against the current. This act can be achieved by stripping in line in a spasmodic fashion, occasionally letting the streamer be washed downstream for a short distance by the current. I have caught more than one larger than average trout by performing this struggling, injured act back and forth by its feeding station.

If imitator patterns don't work, I tie on something highly visible, like a Yellow Marabou Muddler or Mickey Finn to try to entice the fish with big, bold movements in rapid succession. Another deadly technique that can produce trout is to drift a streamer out the downstream end of a riffle, riffles being the primary food producers in most trout streams. The nymphs and small fry that collect in their productive shallows frequently get flushed out the downstream end, where trout wait to gobble them up.

To fish the downstream end of a riffle, position yourself well upstream, out of sight of any trout that may be holding and feeding just below the riffle. You don't even have to make a cast; just strip off line and allow the current to carry your streamer to the back edge of the riffle. When the streamer reaches the end of the riffle, add the theatrics, by stripping line to simulate a minnow that has been flushed off the riffle and is struggling to get back up to it.

At first, allow the fly only to barely drift out of the riffle before it works its way back upstream. On each successive maneuver, allow the fly to drift farther into the deeper water below the riffle, until you have covered all the water downstream from the riffle that looks productive.

If you can resist the temptation of a multitude of runts under ten inches feeding vigorously on an aquatic insect hatch drifting on the surface and have the self-discipline to tie on a streamer, you have a pretty good chance of hooking a fish of bragging proportions. Small trout and even the mature forms of some smaller species of troutstream inhabitants such as chubs and dace will feed on the minute varieties of insects during a hatch. Large trout will also feed on these hatches simultaneously. These larger fish are not above partaking of their smaller brethren during a hatch. Big trout will often lay close to the bottom and take smaller fish that get careless in their enthusiasm to feed on insects floating on the surface.

If you have never fished a streamer under an appreciable number of trout feeding on the surface, no one expects you to ignore the next hatch you encounter and fish a streamer. But give yourself a break the next time you get into a hatch and can't seem to catch anything except runts—just try a streamer for a while under the midgets.

Streamers or bucktails have an inherent advantage over many other types of fly patterns. Since most of them are imitations or suggestions of minnows, it is difficult to fish them in an unrealistic manner. A minnow is liable to appear anywhere in a trout stream, traveling in any direction. Its behavior can vary from drifting dead in the current to making strong upstream surges against the current flow. The key to making streamers most effective is to give them some semblance of life by imparting movement.

Because they may be anywhere in a stream, patterns that imitate minnows are good choices for fishing with a searching technique in large sections of water where you are not sure where fish may be holding. You could do a lot worse than use a streamer or bucktail when you are "fishing the water."

Another prime situation in which the streamer is a good choice occurs when you have been catching a lot of small fish in a particular stream and come upon a section of stream that looks like it should hold fish but no small fish are taken or observed feeding. There is usually a good reason for the sudden scarcity of small fish that were previously so abundant: something big has either chased them off or eaten them. Such a patch of water deserves a long, thorough working with streamers.

Some of the best streamer fishing of the year occurs at the two extreme ends of the season. During the early part of the season, trout don't have the aquatic hatches or large numbers of terrestrials that will be available to them later. Trout also seem to be rather lethargic during the early season, not inclined to expend a lot of effort dashing around on the surface chasing the few early hatching aquatic insects. But they do seem to be susceptible to a streamer fished slowly right down on the bottom.

The end of the season is also prime streamer time. Many of the smaller trout that were in the stream at the beginning of the season have had the whole summer to grow, and many will have increased to a size that permits them to feed on minnows. While these trout were growing in size, some of the other species of minnows in the stream will have brought off hatches and added to the available fry.

In many parts of the country, the end of the season also signals the beginning of the annual spawning. As spawning season approaches, the larger, mature trout become restless and begin to move about more. A highly visible active streamer will often draw a strike when trout are in this fractious frame of mind. A good technique for fishing streamers during this time is to use long casts and cover large areas of water, because a big cruising trout could be almost anywhere just prior to spawning.

The Muddler Minnow is probably the most popular streamer with both trout and trout fishermen, and it is a well-deserved reputation. It can be treated with dry-fly dressing and floated in the surface film to resemble a drowned grasshopper, or it can be weighted and doused with leader sink, then fished right on the bottom, where it resembles several varieties of minnows. It can have the extra added touch of marabou feathers and become a yellow, white, green, red, or black Marabou Muddler. For me the Muddler has produced everything from brown trout inside the city limits of Atlanta to salmon in Alaska.

Another pattern that has gained considerable popularity in the last decade is the Matuka. This pattern comes in a variety of colors, two of my favorites being olive and brown. Unlike most streamer patterns, which are composed primarily of feathers, this one isn't as susceptible to having the feathers become fouled by getting wrapped around the bend of the hook. It also maintains a realistic minnowlike profile in the water.

The Black-Nosed Dace is another pattern common in fly boxes all across the country, because the trout-stream-dwelling minnow it imitates and is named after is common in most North American trout waters.

Some additional patterns that deserve a place in your fly box are the Mickey Finn, Grey Ghost, Dark Edson Tiger, Little Brook

Trout, Little Brown Trout, Little Rainbow Trout, Hornberg, Spruce Fly, Spuddler, Red and White Bucktail, Warden's Worry, and Professor.

This is not intended to be a complete listing of all the streamers you need to fish your particular part of the country but is merely a partial listing of some I have used with fair success. They are a basic selection to get you started if you have not previously been a devotee of the long fly. Local fly shops or tyers could probably give you some good suggestions on rounding out your selection.

12 /

Almost any fly pattern that has a grasshopper silhouette will take trout during mid- to late summer. These four artificials closely resemble the natural insect in the center.

Grasshoppers

ERNEST HEMINGWAY'S TROUT-FISHING STORY "Big Two-Hearted River," long considered a classic short story, is also a classic on piscatorial technique. In the story the hero, Nick Adams, was camping alone and fishing on a stream in Michigan, which many speculate was the Au Sable. Nick caught quite a few fish but lost "the big one."

Did our hero use an immaculately tied clone of some mayfly? No, sir—live grasshoppers. This story reflects an expertise that could have come only from being intimatcly acquainted with the methods of taking trout on grasshoppers. Hemingway's appreciation for the effectiveness of grasshoppers as takers of trout is reflected time and time again in this story.

Another highly respected author in the field of angling literature is Vincent Marinaro, whose *A Modern Dry Fly Code* has enjoyed classic status since it was first published over thirty years ago. The fact that one chapter was devoted to fishing grasshopper imitations may not sound remarkable until you realize that Marinaro proved the worth of his hopper patterns on none other than the famed Letort, probably the most famous of all American limestone streams, renowned for consistent and massive aquatic insect hatches.

The most common grasshoppers (order Orthoptera) are the short-horned variety (family Acrididae), which come in a wide variety of colors and sizes, as do many of the less common varieties. Experience rather than a ten-volume entomological guide to grasshoppers is the key to selecting the most effective hopper patterns for your favorite trout stream.

Hemingway's fictional angler, Nick Adams, was obviously based on a lot of real-life experience in common with that of Vince Marinaro: they both focused on a specific size, shape, and color of grasshopper present in the terrestrial environs adjacent to where they were fishing. Trout frequently feed selectively on a specific model of grasshopper, rejecting just about everything else, so it is important to determine as soon as possible which type of hopper is most common in your section of stream.

In Hemingway's story, Nick caught trout on a stream flowing through a recently burned-over area. He noticed that the hoppers there had taken on a charcoal-tinted hue to camouflage them. I have never collected grasshoppers on the Letort, but after seeing Marinaro's cream-colored hopper pattern that is so deadly on those waters, I'll bet a quart of red ants that the majority of the hoppers there are light in color.

The best time to capture hoppers is very early in the morning when the cool of the day has them somewhat lethargic. As mid-day arrives they become extremely active and agile, making them as difficult to capture as the trout that feed on them. A wide-mouthed terrestrial insect net is handy for capturing hoppers, even in the early morning.

Even after you've secured a good sampling of hoppers, keeping them can be a real exercise in futility. A small jar is handy for holding your captives, but they tend to escape faster than you can put them in. A wad of nylon pantyhose in the bottom of your hopper holder will entangle the spurs on their legs and greatly retard their ability to hop to freedom. Or you may wish to keep captured hoppers in one of those small cricket containers used by bait fishermen.

The importance of grasshoppers as a source of trout food increases with the passing of summer. During the early part of the summer hoppers are not as numerous, as large, or as active as they will be later in the season. As the days become longer and warmer, the activity periods of hoppers will likewise become longer. This increased movement will contribute to their accidentally flying or falling into trout streams with greater regularity. As the hoppers mature, they become capable of longer flights, which also helps account for their frequent inpromptu landings in the drink.

Prime locations for fishing hopper patterns are in sections of stream adjacent to or just downstream from grassy streamside cover, such as a mountain meadow, hayfield, or western grassland. If the grass is located on the upwind side of the prevailing wind, the situation is even more conducive to successful hopper pattern fishing. Taking advantage of a prevailing wind may not seem important to a casual observer, but over the long haul it can play a major role in developing in trout a taste for long-legged snacks. A gentle or moderate prevailing wind won't blast large numbers of hoppers into the stream at any one time. It will, however, tend to work them gradually closer and closer to the stream on each successive flight and eventually deposit a respectable portion of them on the surface of a downwind stream. Brisk, gusty winds, which often accompany a summer shower or storm front, will usually deposit enough grasshoppers in the water to generate some interest in hopper patterns, but even if the wind is dormant, trout will have been feeding on the hoppers earlier and will consider hopper patterns to be prime fare.

Wind is not the only factor that will put enough hoppers in the water to trigger a hopper-feeding binge among the local trout population.

Once when fishing on Castle Creek in South Dakota's Black Hills I was enjoying some pretty good luck with a pattern the locals called a Wonder Nymph, which consisted of a rather slim spun black fur body and two long caudal appendages consisting of white rubber. It didn't look like any natural nymph I had ever seen, and I had tied it on primarily to be polite to my host.

I had been taking a few fish, though on the smallish side. I was working my way upstream, fishing the nymph across and down, when I came around a rise in a small mountain meadow and surprised several dozen half-wild range cattle. As they took off, some walking but some trotting, I speculated that their heavy hoof falls would certainly spook any trout in the promising little stretch of water next to where they had been feeding.

I wanted to give the fish a little time to settle down after that minor stampede, so I sat down to smoke a pipe and enjoy the scenic Black Hills. I was jolted back into reality by a resounding *slurp* that erupted in a smooth slick flowing near the stream bank I was sitting on. As I stared, hoping to locate the rising fish, I noticed a grasshopper struggling in the surface film. He too disappeared—*slurp!* Next two hoppers came drifting down, about a yard and a half apart. The one nearest the stream bank was erased from the surface film with a slurp that was becoming familiar. I clipped off the nymph on my line and had just started tying on a Whitlock Hopper when the remaining hopper of the pair met his doom.

I had guessed that the first trout I had seen rising was working from a feeding station up under the slightly undercut bank and overhanging grass. I cast the hopper upstream of the suspected lie and gently twitched the fly to simulate a struggling grasshopper. The ploy worked: the repetitive slurp became directed at my fly, resulting in a nice eighteen-inch rainbow, followed by several other fish of lesser proportions.

The little meadow soon ended against a thick stand of firs. As I fished into the woods, the hopper ceased to work its magic and I started catching trout only after I switched back to the little black Wonder Nymph with the white rubber tails.

I don't know if the hoppers spooked into the stream by the cattle precipitated an interest in the hopper patterns or if the trout were just naturally conditioned to feeding regularly on grasshoppers in that portion of stream bounded by grass on both sides. I tend to lean toward the latter theory and credit the cattle with attracting my attention to the presence of hoppers in that stream—the trout were probably aware of the hoppers all along.

The first fish I caught in the preceding anecdote was on a feeding station under a slightly undercut bank next to a little run—a prime lie for trout in streams bounded by grassy banks. The combination of undercut bank and overhanging grass offers the type of overhead cover preferred by larger fish, which will position itself in such a lie and defend it against all smaller fish. Such a lie also affords good feeding opportunity, since most of the hoppers and other terrestrials in the grass usually go into the water fairly near the bank.

When fishing a small meadow stream, I like to walk on one bank, fishing upstream ahead of me and across to the other bank. Generally I don't wade in a small stream unless conditions absolutely require it.

These range cattle in the Black Hills flushed a large number of grasshoppers into the small meadow stream in the right of this photo. We followed up the real grasshoppers with artificials and did very well.

If the stream is too large to fish across it efficiently, I'll wade up the middle and cast across and upstream to drift a hopper pattern along undercut banks.

A stream doesn't have to be bounded on both sides by hundreds of acres of western grasslands to be prime hopper-pattern country. Little grassy patches of less than an acre will often harbor enough hoppers to condition nearby trout to feed on them frequently.

The cream-colored Letort Hopper developed by Marinaro, the Whitlock Hopper, and Joe's Hopper can be found in just about any serious fly fisherman's vest. These three patterns have caught trout all over this country and others where hoppers and trout coexist. These standards may not be the best patterns for your favorite trout stream, but no single hopper pattern is probably ideal for different stretches of the same stream.

It doesn't require a radical new fly pattern to duplicate one or more of the common hoppers found on your favorite waters—just take one of the excellent standard hopper patterns, such as the three just mentioned, and use a body material of the same color as the natural. You may want to tie one or two in all-green materials to simulate the hoppers present on leafy green vegetation.

Hoppers are just about the easiest patterns to fish successfully, because grasshoppers have just about the most versatile aquatic repertoires of any terrestrial insect. They respond to an impromptu dunking in many different ways. Some swim in erratic patterns with a strong froglike kicking stroke, others spread their wings slightly as if to fly back to land, and some seem resigned to their fate and are content just to drift listlessly in the current.

Since a hopper floating in the film of a stream behaves so erratically, you can fish an imitation in a dead drift, with slight twitches, or like a freshly dunked insect swimming strongly on the surface.

I usually like first to offer a hopper to a feeding fish or place it near a suspected feeding station in a dead drift. If several dead drifts don't produce, I'll add a few seductive twitches as it drifts in the current. If neither of these tactics produce, I twitch the fly vigorously as it drifts past a suspected lie. By using the gentle dead drift first and gradually progressing up to a more vigorous presentation, there is less chance of spooking a cautious fish.

Do not assume that because a trout may not be particular about how he takes his hoppers you can be sloppy in your approach and presentation. Trout flies, no matter how strongly they are worked, don't spook fish, but sloppy casting, heavy-footed walking on stream banks, careless wading, and skylighted anglers will turn them off right away.

The importance of maintaining a low profile when fishing from grassy areas cannot be overemphasized. This usually low-level vegetation affords little cover to break up a fisherman's outline and mask his movements, so stay low.

An effective cast to use with the hopper, especially in fast-moving water with a slightly broken surface, is one that delivers the fly to the surface with a satisfying little splat. A big juicy hopper doesn't light on the surface with the finesse of a size-28 Light Cahill; he lands like a B-29 of the bug world. Don't splat your whole line against the water, just the fly. Aiming your cast high and giving the rod tip a slight backward twitch just as the fly reaches the end of the leader will cause the fly to flip down against the surface and the line will settle gently, as it does with a normal cast.

One of the best places to fish grasshopper patterns is right up next to a grassy stream bank.

The same wind that deposits hoppers in the water and contributes to your successful use of this pattern can also play havoc with your casting distance and accuracy. The higher the wind, the better the hopper fishing and the tougher the casting. The aerodynamics of a big bushy hopper pattern further compound the problem. A weight-forward line is minimal equipment for flicking hopper patterns in the winds that are present on most western streams where these patterns are at their very best. I even keep a few bug tapers and saltwater tapers in my kit for when it really blows.

Again, how you fish a hopper pattern is not ultracritical, but where you fish it can be a different story. When trout are up under a grassy bank slurping hoppers off the surface, a brisk wind can make it mighty difficult to lay a fly right up near or under the grass where the big boys have set up housekeeping. It takes a weight-forward line and a heavy leader to place big hopper patterns where they need to be.

Do not confine your hopper fishing just to large western streams or even streams that flow predominantly through meadowlands. Some excellent hopper fishing can be had even on tiny streams you can almost jump across. As streams decrease in size, terrestrial food organisms usually increase in importance. As the volume of aquatic habitat decreases, the ratio of streamside habitat increases. Consequently, a relatively small section of grass on the bank of a small stream can influence the feeding patterns of trout living in it.

Another characteristic of fish in small streams is that they must of necessity feed in an opportunistic pattern more often than they normally would, if not perpetually. Since these small streams severely restrict casting room even when they have just a bit of streamside vegetation, it may become necessary to dap hopper patterns on the surface, using a long rod from behind some streamside concealment.

A selection of hopper patterns including sizes 12, 10, 8, and 6 will be adequate for most situations, though there may be grasshopper populations on some of your favorite streams that would require larger patterns. The smaller sizes are usually best during the early part of the summer, since the naturals are generally smaller then.

A little hopper research can go a long way toward your obtaining maximum potential from these patterns. A little time and energy spent collecting grasshoppers from grassy areas along a stream you intend to fish will be rewarded. The human hand can in a pinch serve to capture hoppers, but the success ratio can be meager on a warm day when the hoppers are agile and active.

Any trout fisherman worth his dry-fly dope should have a net for collecting insects. (Mine has a nasty habit of being someplace where I'm not.) I use a tight-mesh landing net that can be pressed into service as an insect-capturing net that will tangle up anything but the smallest insects. It is not ideal for collecting specimens, but it sure is better than using my hands. To increase efficiency further and reduce frustration, an improvised extension handle in the form of a stick can be lashed or taped to the handle of the net.

In addition to determining the predominant size and color of local hoppers, your education can be enhanced if you take a collection of hoppers to a stream and toss them in to observe the consequences. To obtain maximum realism with your artificials, study how a hopper hits the water, its various reactions, and how it floats in various currents.

It is worth also noting how trout take grasshoppers. I have noticed during this exercise that trout will often make a false strike at the larger sizes of natural grasshoppers and hopper patterns, frequently bumping larger versions vigorously before actually taking them. This prestrike bump often triggers a hook-set by the angler that misses. It is hard to do, but it is a good idea to try to be certain that a rising fish has actually taken a large-size hopper pattern before you set the hook. This is hard to do and takes no small amount of self-control, but if you can avoid setting the hook on that first false rise, you will get a positive strike, right after which your quarry will be hooked. Fortunately, this "bump before you strike" behavior seems to be most common with larger patterns that are highly visible, which makes it easier to identify a false rise.

Another member of the grasshopper clan bears mentioning, since the insects and the patterns that imitate them are so similar, and that is the cricket. I have rarely seen a cricket in a trout's stomach or netted one out of a stream with a nymph seine. I do know of a brown once that went over twelve pounds that was caught on a live cricket within the city limits of Atlanta, and know that Ed Koch set a dry-fly record for Pennsylvania with a nine-pound trout taken on a cricket pattern. The Letort Cricket (tied identical to the Letort Hopper except that the Hopper is tan and the cricket is black) developed by Vince Marinaro years ago continues to be one of the most popular patterns in the Pennsylvania limestone country legendary for aquatic insect hatches. With a track record (creek record?) like that, cricket patterns must have something that appeals to trout.

Since crickets are not a food item that is frequently available to trout, much of this pattern's attraction must rest on its simplicity and the fact that it resembles several of the terrestrial species that trout feed on, such as dark grasshoppers, beetles, and large horseflies. It may be, after all, one of those suggestive patterns that doesn't resemble anything specific but just looks like something that would please a trout's palate.

I leave the rationale and explanation for this pattern's effectiveness up to more learned minds; all I know is that this pattern has produced for me on a lot of different trout waters under many different situations.

13/

Trying to align the sections of a fly rod in the dark by following the guides can be impossible when it is too dark to see your rod tip. To avoid this aggravation, mark the two parts of the rod ferrules with dots of white paint. The dots are easy to see in poor light and will eliminate the need to shine a flashlight near a stream at night.

Things That Go Splash in the Night

A LOT OF FISHERMEN talk about the big trout that can be caught after dark, but few do anything about it. I am amazed at how few anglers fish for trout at night, even though it is common knowledge that many large trout (especially browns) are primarily nocturnal and do most, if not all, of their feeding between dusk and dawn. Even in streams that are subjected to intensive fishing pressure, some fish survive long enough to obtain monster proportions by being nocturnal.

One of my greatest pleasures in trout fishing is just being on the stream. Like the alcoholic who has never tasted any bad whiskey, I have never seen an ugly trout stream. Night fishing eliminates any possibility of enjoying the trout-stream scenery I love so much, but it makes up for this loss in a tingling anticipation I don't get during daylight fishing. From the moment I step into the stream until I leave it hours later, I expect something big and exciting to happen. More often than not I don't catch any fish, but when I do it makes up for all those fishless nights, because I don't fish for yearling trout at night, I fish for the trout—the "cannibal brown"—that eat the yearlings!

Night fishing is not necessarily difficult, nor does it require skills beyond the abilities of the average fly fisherman, but it does require some radical modifications in how you fish and what you fish with. About the only similarity between daytime trout fishing and night fishing is that you use a fly rod for both. Just about everything else is different, including the type and size of fly, the casting technique, and leader length and size. Even reading the water you expect to fish takes on new dimensions and detail never required for daylight trout fishing.

You can bet that any stream you have ever fished that had brown trout in it had some real lunkers in it, however much fishing pressure it was subjected to. In fact, intensive daytime fishing pressure often contributes to excellent night fishing. A steady parade of heavy-footed fishermen will put a big brown off his feed and up under the nearest cover, where he'll stay until the herd goes home at the end of the day. Only after the commotion has subsided will he venture from cover and begin to feed.

I have never fished a stream at night that I had not previously fished in daylight or at least thoroughly scouted before dark. As a general rule, I don't "fish the water" after dark. In most cases I concentrate on just one or two locations I know or suspect to hold large fish. The patch of target water may have been selected because I saw a large fish in the area during daylight. Have you ever located a big trout and showed him everything in your fly box without his ever showing any interest at all? You can bet that tight-lipped monster is waiting for the sun to go down before he starts grocery shopping.

Have you ever located what appeared to be a prime lie for a big trout but couldn't catch even a small fish there? If you have had more than a little trout-fishing experience and have learned to recognize good trout habitat, you have probably guessed correctly about the presence of a big trout, but your mistake was that you gave up on him after you couldn't catch him in broad daylight on a size-16 hatch matcher. Whenever you encounter prime water and don't catch even a few small fish, you should begin to consider the possibility of a large nocturnal feeder. If you fish the stream often and consistently take fish above or below this good-looking patch of water, you can almost be assured that a big trout is in residence.

Even if you have fished a similar spot on your favorite stream frequently in daylight, you need to give it a long, hard look. To begin your night-fishing career you need to consider such details as where you will enter the stream, find several locations to cast from, check the current flow patterns, and find feeding stations and underwater obstacles or snags that may interfere with fly or line. Only after you have thoroughly scouted a section of stream can you hope to fish that water effectively in the dark. Wading in the dark and casting at random is an exercise fraught with risk and frustration.

I adhere to the philosophy that big fish eat big food and that nocturnal feeders are practically addicted to this practice. Most of the serious night fishermen I know are so convinced that big night-feeding fish prefer their grub in large hunks that they rarely fish a fly under size 6. The preference of both night-feeding fish and night-fishing anglers is size 4 or larger.

Few would argue that big trout that feed only at night live long enough to reach large proportions because they don't feed when fishermen are on the stream to catch them: if they aren't feeding when anglers are fishing, they don't get caught, which is conducive to longevity and bulk. I would also postulate that they get big because they have a preference for large food. The net nutritional gain from capturing a single thumb-sized crayfish, a five-inch fish, or some other food organism of heroic proportions must be greater than the net nutritional gain achieved by making fifty trips after fifty individual midges. One trip after something big should put more weight on a fish than many trips after tiny morsels, even if the trips are short. I have taken too many large food items out of the stomachs of large night-feeding trout to harbor many doubts about their propensity for taking their nourishment in bulk.

There may be an advantage in using larger fly patterns at night which are easier for a trout to see and strike under low light conditions. This is of particular importance when you realize that the best night fishing usually occurs when there is no moon and the cloud cover eliminates starlight.

A trout should also be able to hear a fly if he is to locate it under poor light conditions. Trout have two sets of ears with which to locate prey by sounds. One is a set of internal ears located in the top of the head, which have no external openings but can detect vibrations through the skin, bone, and flesh of the head. The other hearing system is an organ called the lateral line, which runs from the fish's tail along his side and down his lower jaw. This collection of specialized cells picks up vibrations to help trout locate prey. These highly sophisticated organs are aided in their function by the fact that sound travels through water five times faster than through air.

Some experienced night fishermen use cork-bodied surface bugs of the type normally used by bass fishermen. I have never had very much luck with this style of fly, but some swear by it.

For top-water work I like size 4 or larger grasshopper patterns because they create enough surface disturbance for a night feeder to find them, but they don't produce the excessive disruption when picked up off the water that bass bugs sometimes do. A Muddler pattern heavily dressed on a thin wire hook will work well as a top-water fly when dressed with dry-fly floatant.

The Muddler is also one of my favorites for working deep. The White Marabou Muddler, weighted, has been one of the better producers for me. If you don't trim the deer-hair head quite as closely as the standard Muddler design, the extra strands of stiff deer hair will create a little extra "noise" as the fly is retrieved along the bottom. The lifelike swimming action and increased visibility provided by the white marabou feathers help the fish pinpoint the fly and add realistic movement.

Jim Bashline, the most dedicated and accomplished night trout fisherman I know, has written the excellent *Night Fishing for Trout*. Jim advocates using large wet flies, sizes 4 to 8, such as the Silver Doctor, Governor, Professor, Queen of the Waters, and Alexandra. You won't find these old standards mentioned in much of the current trout-fishing literature. The nocturnal Mr. Bashline was responsible for my experimenting with these old standard wet flies; he knew what he was talking about.

Another technique that seemed radical at the time Jim told me about it has also proven to be deadly with night-feeding trout. Jim fishes wet flies on droppers, two and three at a time. I kid him about fishing with "coveys of flies," but he insists that he can always tell where his backcast is going because he can hear those big wet flies swooshing over his head in formation. Fishing two or three wet flies in the middle of the night sounded foolish, so I harassed Jim about it unmercifully—until I tried it. I'm sure it won't seem ridiculous at all to you once you try it. If there are some oldtimers around who have fished with the standard wet-fly patterns, find out which flies produced and try them on one of Jim's multiple wet-fly rigs.

The leaders need not be long or fine for night fishing. A tapered leader with at least an eight-pound tippet is about as small as you need to go, with a ten- or twelve-pound tippet being better choices. The heavier tippets allow more control with larger fly patterns and droppers. The additional strength is also a welcome advantage when you are trying to keep a big brown out from under tree roots along the bank or to restrain his flight to the next county.

Frequent hook inspections and touchups with a whetstone are a good idea. The larger hook sizes will penetrate better if you keep them sharp. No matter how well you know the water you will be fishing in the dark, expect some hangups. After each such episode, check hook points for a possible sharpening.

Long-distance casting is not often possible or practical when fishing with one or more large flies in the dark. Accurate long-range casting with a big-weighted Muddler or several size-4 wets can be a real character builder, even in the daylight. If you have scouted the water before dark, you should have selected a casting position that will allow you to work the water where you expect a big fish to be without having to make excessively long casts.

Since most of your casts will be relatively short, cautious wading is important. Careless wading that disturbs rocks and creates a disturbance is just as detrimental to fishing at night as during the day. The lack of illumination may reduce a trout's chances of seeing you somewhat, but darkness sure won't impair his hearing.

For most of my night fishing I use an eight-and-a-half-foot graphite fly rod and an AFTMA 8-weight line. This rod and line combination permit me to handle the larger flies with a little more authority than a shorter rod with a 5- or 6-weight line.

Fly-casting technique and methods of fishing flies after they are in the water are pretty much a matter of individual skill and preference. It would be difficult indeed to find two fly fishermen who cast exactly the same or even work a drifting fly the same. Add to these individual characteristics regional preferences and the inconsistent nomenclature with which we describe our techniques and the opportunities for confusion are unlimited.

Except in those streams where the geographical configuration eliminates any choice, I like to cast across stream and down when work-ing a big fish at night. After a few such casts I can let out a little more line and cover some new water and can systematically fish the water ahead of me as I gradually creep downstream. Keeping slack out of your line and following the position of your fly after casting upstream is a maneuver I have never been able to execute successfully in the dark. The "down and across" has been by far the most practical cast and drift to control.

After the fly has drifted downstream and swung across in the cur-rent, I retrieve it straight back upstream, either by stripping line in between the fingers of the hand gripping the rod or using a hand twist retrieve. A good percentage of the fish I have taken at night, on both wet and dry flies, have taken the fly during such an upcurrent retrieve.

In the waters most of us fish, big trout are rare, so when you have one located and are trying to catch him at night, don't give up too soon. Sometimes a big trout may not even begin to start feeding until several hours after dark or maybe not until an hour or two before daylight. If you have a fish located, stay with him. If after trying several dozen casts and a variety of flies you don't get any action, rest yourself and the fish. Take a coffee break and go sit down for a while—but don't give up if you know that fish is in the area.

I have read and heard about night fishermen who tie on flies in the dark without the aid of a light. I am enormously impressed, because that is a feat I have never been able to master, even when my eyes were younger and could see a lot better than they can now. I keep one of those miniature flashlights that use only one small penlight battery on a lanyard around my neck for changing flies at night. I can hold it between my teeth, which frees both hands for work. With the light in my teeth, I keep my chin pressed hard against my chest, which causes the light to shine against the front of my vest, not cast light directly on the water. I turn my back to where I think the fish is before turning the light on. If I am just finishing a coffee break or a rest, I'll move well away from the stream and make any necessary fly changes before entering the water again. Of course I keep a regular two-cell flashlight in a large pocket in the back of my vest for those emergencies when I need some real light to untangle a fish, my line, or myself.

When I first started night fishing, getting the guides aligned on a two-piece rod was a chore at best and nearly impossible on one of those pack rods that come in sections about as long as chopsticks. To reduce aggravation during tackle assembly, I sat down one evening and assembled every jointed rod I had. After joining all the rods I took some white paint and put a small dot on each half of the ferrule so that now all I have to do is line up the two white dots. No more holding a rod up toward the sky, trying to eyeball the guides to see if they are properly aligned! Using these marks also speeds up rod assembly in daylight.

Caterpillar patterns are effective during those times of the year when the naturals are available to trout. The presence of just one or two caterpillars on streamside vegetation is reason enough to tie on a fly of this type, since there are probably many other naturals around that you don't see.

Caterpillars

CATERPILLARS, inchworms, leaf rollers, oak worms, and measuring worms are just a few of the names applied to these immature terrestrial insects that trout relish. Like many other terrestrial food forms, these also reach peak populations at certain times of the year, during which imitations are most effective.

It doesn't require an insect collecting net or a magnifying glass to discover the presence of caterpillars. Some varieties, which hang suspended on almost invisible silk threads, are often encountered as you travel along stream banks. Since the adults lay eggs in clusters that number in the hundreds, it is a safe assumption that any caterpillars you observe near a stream will have many siblings in the immediate vicinity that you may not have seen. The presence of several caterpillars of a given species should trigger your use of a matching artificial. Caterpillar imitations are most effective when there is a good bit of overhanging vegetation on a stream. Don't look for this vegetation only near ground level, for many caterpillars fall from great heights, such as the tops of tall deciduous trees.

Caterpillars are prime trout fare for several reasons. They are relatively large, providing a substantial mass of food, compared with other trout foods such as midges. Caterpillars also are easy to catch, since they are poor swimmers and merely drift along in the current. Finally, they are periodically available in substantial numbers.

The existence of caterpillars in large numbers can stimulate a selective feeding pattern among trout in those sections of a stream where a particular species is abundant. A trout feeding selectively on a specific caterpillar may not be as difficult to fool as one feeding selectively on an adult aquatic insect. The adult will be of a uniform size, shape, and color, which must be duplicated with some degree of accuracy. However, caterpillars of the same species usually start off small and increase in size by gluttonous feeding on leafy vegetation. Usually it is sufficient to imitate color and shape, with size being not quite so important.

Some—in fact, many—caterpillars are what entomologists call "host selective," meaning that they feed only on one specific type of plant, such as chickweed, ferns, or catawba trees. One caterpillar is commonly known as an oak worm, since it frequently hangs by a single silk strand from the tree of that name.

I once contacted an entomologist with the U.S. Fish and Wildlife Service to identify a specific caterpillar I knew only as a "sour wood-worm," a species greatly prized by bait fishermen on streams in the southern Appalachians. During our conversation I discovered that there were over 150 species of moths of the family Geometridae in my area. Once again I came to the conclusion that to match a specific insect form may not be as desirable as being prepared with patterns that resemble several similar forms.

Inchworm patterns are simple in design; even the most ungifted fly tyer can produce them. They require only a small bunch of deer hair tied parallel to the shank of a long-shanked hook. The ends of the deer hair are then clipped off behind the eye and bend of the hook. Several sizes should be tied, with colors to match the most common caterpillars in your area. My own assortment includes colors in natural brown deer hair as well as deer hair dyed yellow, pale green, lime green, olive, and chartreuse. Some fly tyers put elaborate bends and curves in the hook shanks prior to tying an inchworm pattern, but I have not found this necessary.

Inchworm patterns can also be constructed by wrapping the hook shank with chenille in various colors to duplicate some of the common varieties. To add further realism for the woolly types, just add a Palmer hackle on top of the chenille. Of course, when you tie up a caterpillar like this a purist will argue that you no longer have a caterpillar pattern but instead one of the standard Wooly Worm patterns; he would be right.

I have often wondered if the coast-to-coast deserved popularity of the Wooly Worm has not been due in some part to its close similarity to a woolly caterpillar-type worm. Piscatorial practitioners have justified the effectiveness of the Wooly Worm because it theoretically resembles everything from stonefly nymphs to hellgrammites (larvae of the Dobson fly). There are those who would argue that the Wooly Worm resembles some food form specifically, which may be true (I am sure it occasionally is), but I am also convinced that the Wooly Worm is deadly on streams from coast to coast because it resembles several food forms and duplicates a woolly caterpillar more than any other single food item consumed by trout.

Peak caterpillar populations and top activity periods for some species may span only a few weeks and may occur any time from late spring until fall, depending on where you do your trout fishing. One of the major keys to making the caterpillar pattern work for you is to observe carefully the streamside vegetation for sample specimens, then use a similar pattern.

A pattern's behavior in a stream can often supply a clue as to which version of a caterpillar is currently plentiful. Some of the hairy models will float for a while, suspended by the hairs on their bodies in much the same way the hackle supports a dry fly. Most of the smooth-bodied types float like an 00 buck and sink like a split shot. The floating types are fairly easy to see, but sometimes the darker colored varieties are mistaken for a piece of forest duff that has gotten into the stream and not been recognized as a potential food organism for trout. If the floating caterpillar is brightly hued or of a multicolored pattern, it is usually easily recognizable as an insect.

Another location that should be carefully scrutinized during caterpillar season is where shallow waters flow over moss-covered rocks or ledges. Some varieties of aquatic moss are stiff and short. The claws of a caterpillar, which are designed for clinging to plants, will often catch on underwater vegetation and cause a drowned caterpillar to become caught. They adhere so well that sometimes when you pull an entangled caterpillar off a moss-covered rock it is not unlike separating one of those Velcro closures so popular on modern fishing vests. Carefully inspecting these moss-covered rocks will often reveal not only which caterpillars are abundant, but also which are currently active and getting into the stream. Again, reading a stream must be a continuous process, focusing on many places, not just the water's surface. If you make it a habit to inspect carefully all submerged moss for snagged caterpillars, you will find this occurrence to be far from rare.

The dead drift method is by far the most realistic one for fishing caterpillar patterns. You may want to add a few small split shot at the barrel knots of your leader. A good dose of leader sink on the fly will also assist in keeping inchworms on or very near the bottom, where most of the drowned naturals are found.

I keep in my fly vest several types of Wooly Worm patterns, which are tied on wire hooks and have extra Palmer hackles applied to help keep them on the surface. This extra hackle is a deviation from the standard pattern, but it does help keep my fly on top, and the extra hackle adds to the realistic appearance of the woolly-type inchworms that are the only ones that float in their natural form.

Frequently, inchworms can be observed hanging from streamside vegetation on a single strand of silk. When this is observed, it is a good idea to cast through one of the strands to observe whether the natural floats or sinks and its drift route. Occasionally you will be rewarded by seeing a fish take the natural. This will remove many unknowns in the trout-catching equation. You will know what they are hitting, how to fish it, and approximately where the feeding station is. You can even sweeten the pot by cutting several strands with a sweeping side cast and stimulating active feeding with the inchworm "chum" that drifts downstream.

Like most other crawling types of terrestrials (as opposed to the winged varieties), most of the caterpillars will be found near shore and downstream of overhanging streamside vegetation, except where a strong meandering current sweeps them into midstream. It is a good idea to be alert for a strong cross-stream current that is downstream from overhanging vegetation and its accompanying inchworms. In these circumstances, it is quite possible that a trout in midstream, on station near the crossing current, may be feeding selectively on caterpillars that came into the stream near shore just a short distance upstream.

In a strong cross-stream current downstream from overhanging vege-
tation, trout may be feeding selectively on caterpillars that came into
the stream near shore a short distance upstream.

15

Most wet flies have soft hen-feather hackles and are designed to absorb water and sink fast. The soft hackle used in these flies also produces a lifelike appearance in the water.

Wet Flies

THE TERM "WET FLIES" could be applied to any pattern fished below the surface, including nymphs and streamers, so to avoid confusion let me classify as a wet fly any of those patterns that are tied with soft hackle and have absorbent bodies and wings that slant back over the fly body at a forty-five-degree angle or less.

The modern fly fisherman may have a score of fly boxes loaded with the latest editions of hatch-matcher miracle patterns constructed from poly-this or poly-that but may be found wanting when it comes to having a few of the old, time-proven wet patterns. One advantage of civilization (the only?) is that one generation can pass on what it has learned, but the current generation of fly fishermen has tended to ignore the lessons learned by its predecessors, such respected outdoor scribes as Ed Zern, Jim Bashline, A. J. McClane, Tom McNally, and others.

All wet flies may not have wings—some of them may consist simply of a soft, absorbent body and a hackle made of a hen's neck feather. A partial list of these old patterns would include those listed on page 133.

Many of these patterns can be ordered from some of the larger mail-order suppliers. You will have to look close to find them, because they rarely occupy a prominent place in catalogs. If you want to produce your own flies, I strongly recommend two fly-tying volumes by the renowned J. Edson Leonard, whose *Flies* has been a standard on fly patterns and how to tie them since it was first published in 1950. Ed's most recent book, *The Essential Fly Tier*, has also earned well-deserved accolades. Both works contain valuable information on how to tie many varieties of wet flies.

I have had the enviable experience of observing Ed Leonard on the business end of both a fly rod and a fly-tying vise. His appreciation of the wet fly was evident in both endeavors. Ed ties his wet patterns with five basic characteristics: sparseness, absorption, profile, and color—all on a heavy hook, to facilitate fast sinking.

When I was being considered for Southern Field Editor at *Field & Stream* magazine, Ed Zern came down to my home to interview me and do some fishing. We began our expedition on Waters Creek in the Chattahoochee National Forest, a trophy-trout stream that probably has the largest minimum size limit in the country: rainbows and browns must be over twenty-two inches, brookies over eighteen inches, and you may keep only one fish per day.

I took Ed to a pool I knew held several "keeper" browns. Looking like two cat burglars, we sneaked up to the pool and I directed Ed's attention to a shadow underneath a partly submerged log lying perpendicular to the stream. Ed immediately spotted a large brown that was definitely over the twenty-two-inch minimum lying under the end of the log toward our side of the stream. "I never dreamed there was a brown trout that size in Georgia!" I waited, but said nothing, because I knew there was more to come. "Look! There's another one, lying just to his left!" . . . "My God, there's another . . . and another . . . and another!" There were at least half a dozen big trout under that one log.

Ed quickly contracted a severe case of brown trout "buck fever" and promptly forgot he was there to watch me fish. I suggested he try them, but he declined politely. When I offered again Ed could resist no longer.

We retreated from the edge of the stream for Ed to rig up and tie on a fly. With trembling fingers he tied on a wet fly I didn't recognize. "It's called a Dickey Fly," he said. As he finished knotting the fly to his tippet, I made a mental note to find out more about this fly, which was *Field & Stream*'s Fishing Editor's first choice when confronted with a pool full of trophy-dimension browns.

Ed connected with one of those lunkers in fewer than a dozen casts. Through no fault of his own, he lost that big one, and later another broke off by dashing up under some exposed tree roots below the bank. I bummed a Dickey from Ed and also hooked into a

Pattern	Recommended Sizes
Leadwing Coachman	10,12,14
Light Cahill	12,14
Gold-Ribbed Hare's Ear	10,12,14
Parmachene Belle	10,12,14
Dark Cahill	12,14
Professor	12,14
Silver Doctor	10,12,14
Royal Coachman	10,12,14
Brown Hackle	12,14
Cowdung	10,12,14

big fish that broke me off—Waters Creek is small and strewn with obstacles that can quickly break a leader.

On the trip home that evening Ed reflected on how many fishermen could fly fish a whole lifetime without tying into three browns the way we had that single afternoon. We lost our big fish, but I made a substantial catch in the Dickey Fly.

Later Ed gave me his formula for tying the Dickey. He ties it on a number 6, 3X-long light-wire hook, then fashions a cotton-batting body or wraps wool on the hook shank. Next he covers the body base with peacock herl and then a gold rib, after which comes a dun hen-hackle at the head.

Since that first introduction to the Dickey Fly, I have caught trout with it in Alaska, Vermont, South Dakota, New Mexico, Tennessee, North Carolina, and Georgia. The pattern has that special something that makes it appealing: with it I have caught rainbows, browns, cutthroat, brookies, and Dolly Vardens. The Dickey doesn't duplicate any specific form of trout food I know about, but it must look like something good for trout to eat.

The suggestiveness inherent in the Dickey Fly is typical of the wet fly breed as a whole. Some would argue that wet flies imitate drowned aquatics or terrestrials of one form or another, and it would be easy to debate the resemblance of a wet fly to an emerging mayfly or caddis. Ed Leonard did some impressive work on one of our trips with a size-12 caddis pattern that he soaked with leader sink and fished wet!

Back when the wet fly was in its prime, Ed Zern used them three at a time by tying two droppers on his leader. The point or terminal fly was always the Dickey. About twenty-five inches up the leader he attached the first dropper, to which was affixed a number 12 Leadwing Coachman. About twenty inches up from the middle dropper Ed attached the second dropper, which had a Royal Coachman tied wet in a size 12 or 14. The white wing in the Coachman, which was fairly visible, served as a strike indicator of sorts.

For those of you not familiar with tying droppers, the process is quite simple. When you tie up a leader, just allow for the heavier of the two line segments to have enough tag sticking out to make a dropper about ten to twelve inches long. Clip off the smaller diameter line right at the knot, but leave the long section of heavier line for the dropper. After tying up a few leaders with droppers, you'll find it just as easy and fast as tying a regular leader.

If you have some leaders already made up, you can add droppers by simply attaching the dropper above a blood knot (which is already in your leader) with a clinch knot. Using a clinch knot in this way makes it quite easy to improvise droppers on your leader.

To those who have never tried casting a line with three flies on it, it may sound cumbersome. It is at first—and sounds a lot worse than it casts! Three wet flies sailing by your ears produces a "whoosh" overhead that is not unlike the sound that would be created by a ten-pound honeybee, but with a little practice the three-fly rig isn't difficult to cast. In fact, I had more trouble learning to cast a Weighted Muddler than I did wet flies on droppers. You may want just to start off with a single terminal fly and a single dropper before trying to master two droppers.

Once you have mastered how to cast a trio of wet flies, you must resolve where to cast them. Just about anything that works with a single wet fly will work with three, such as casting across the stream and executing the standard wet-fly swing. After the flies have drifted directly downstream you can retrieve them by stripping in line with short four- or five-inch tugs. By lifting your rod tip high during this upstream stripping retrieve you can position the top dropper fly near the surface or actually skate it across the surface, which often triggers a vigorous strike. Most of the fish I have taken on this top fly skating on the surface have been on the smallish side.

If you feel that quite a deep drift is necessary, you may want to cast upstream with a slack-line cast, to allow the trio of flies to get down close to the bottom before they drift through what you know or suspect to be prime water. To make the slack-line cast with a trio of wet flies, just overpower your forward cast and stop your rod tip at the eleven-o'clock position. This maneuver will cause the line to straighten out completely and then fall back toward you, landing on the water in a slack configuration.

Many anglers who are just starting to fish multiple flies on droppers are intimidated by underwater obstacles such as exposed tree roots. Of course you will get hung up more often when fishing three flies than just one, as you drift those flies under banks. But flies are the fisherman's cheapest equipment, even at approximately a dollar a fly, and you will get hung on a trout often enough to make the risk worthwhile.

You may want occasionally to mix up your fly patterns to give your quarry a three-way multiple choice. Experiment with sizes or colors to find out what is working and what isn't. To use this process of elimination, you could start off with three size 10 flies in three different patterns or colors, which would give a trout, say, a brown, a cream, and an olive-colored fly to choose from. Then you could progressively increase or decrease the size until something produced. More often than not you will get fish on several different patterns during the day. As a general rule, more fish will be taken over the long haul if you use patterns that are significantly different in color, size, or shape.

Fishing wet flies can be the most relaxing form of fly fishing I know. When I have flailed the water with every dry fly and nymph in the box and nothing has worked (in spite of what some would have you believe this does happen to authors of fly-fishing books!), I go to my "low anxiety" technique of tying on three wets, casting across the stream, and letting the flies drift until the line becomes taut. I take three or four steps downstream, then repeat the process. This is not only a relaxing way to fish but is often productive.

One of the biggest problems with casting three wets at the same time is getting them near or on the surface before beginning the back cast. To generate maximum energy on the back cast (which is the power stroke, and not the forward cast, as some fishermen believe), I extend my casting arm almost straight, then bend it at the elbow and bring my elbow sharply to my side. This precast maneuver takes slack out of the line and loads the rod prior to actually starting the back cast that will lift the line and flies off the water. This is an old southern bass-bugging move, but it works nicely for lifting a flight of wet flies off the water.

It may well be my imagination, but it seems to me that on the average I get larger trout on wet flies, except when I skate the top dropper on the surface. This may be due to a trout's, especially a wise old big 'un, believing that a drifting wet fly may be easier to catch than some frisky dry fly floating on the surface. I sure would hate to have to make a living catching something as active as an adult caddis that had just emerged into an adult. When they hatch, they don't even pause on the surface but just seem to fly right out of the water like a flying fish in the ocean, which is one reason I try to work wets as sluggishly as possible, which seems to work rather well.

A. J. McClane has confessed his addiction to fishing wets in multiples on numerous occasions, and he also apparently subscribes to the philosophy that wets should appear to be easy to catch. After he has cast a pair of wet flies and allowed them to drift downstream, he allows them to remain motionless in the current for twenty seconds or longer. That may not seem like long, but if you look at your watch for twenty seconds and imagine that your fly has just completed its drift at the beginning of that period, you will realize that you are pulling your flies out for the next cast too soon.

Polaroid glasses are not only a valuable asset for detecting fish feeding below the surface but are also helpful in seeing a fish take one of your wets.

You should use the stiffest leader material you can find when fishing wets on droppers. The construction of the flies themselves will contribute to some weird movements in fast water. The really fine or flexible leader material will result in nothing but leader tangles and profanity.

I don't expect anyone who has been brainwashed by all the current literature on exact duplication to discard all his Latin-named fly patterns and rush to his favorite stream with his leader sporting droppers with wet flies. But I do suggest that you put a few wets in your fly box and the next time you don't have a hatch to match, tie on a few wets and have some fun catching fish.

16/

This angler was successful on a cold, foggy morning when he had no hatch to match.

Potpourri:
From Bees
to Beetles

ONE OF THE FAVORITE PASTIMES of the older natives in my section of the Appalachians is finding wild-bee trees in the springtime to locate wild-bee colonies. These oldsters don't use any of the fancy baits or lures to attract bees and then "course" them back to the hive by watching their direction of flight; they just walk along a mountain stream and carefully watch every gravel bar or sandbar. As you know, bees have very short legs and don't swim any better than a trout flies, so they must supply themselves with water in shallow— *very* shallow—depths; hence their preference for gravel- and sandbars. Another peculiarity of these social insects is that they will always collect water at the closest source and the entire force of workers will use that spot.

By now you have figured out why this is important to the trout fisherman. Bees are numerous—a single hive may contain sixty thousand individuals—and very active. With this many insects collecting water at the same spot, it is easy to understand why trout on the downstream side of a hive's watering location soon become accustomed to feeding on bees. Trout rarely get enough bees at one time to stimulate a selective feeding pattern, but they do eat bees as the opportunity presents itself, in a random but regular routine. This might be called preferential feeding, as opposed to selective or opportunistic feeding patterns.

To locate one of these bee-watering sites, keep your eyes open for something other than mayflies or caddis flies. Make it a point to scrutinize for bees each gravel- and sandbar you pass. They won't come in a large, highly visible swarm, but as single insects. Look for them right at the water's edge.

That old standard, the McGinty Bee, is as good a pattern as you will find for drifting through the holding water downstream from the location where bees quench their thirst.

Another insect that gets into a lot of trouble around water is the yellowjacket. These pugnacious characters require a lot of water, for brood rearing and nest construction. If you want to see just how poor a swimmer a yellowjacket is, hang a small fish over a bucket of water, with the fish just barely above the surface of the water. In late summer or early fall, yellowjackets will cover up that fish to suck its fluids and eat its flesh. Apparently they forget that they have added some weight since landing, because when they depart they inevitably swerve downward and land in the water, where they promptly drown. (We use this technique around our house to reduce the yellowjacket populations; just dip the carcasses out of the bucket every hour or so, to keep the late arrivals from walking to safety on floating dead bodies.)

Obviously, the presence of the fish attracts yellowjackets in greater numbers than those in which they would collect and drown on a trout stream. But when yellowjackets are present, they are there in great numbers, so it is logical to assume that many of them will accidentally get into a trout stream, where trout will take them. A sparsely dressed McGinty Bee makes a good yellowjacket pattern.

If you are ever camped next to a stream during the peak of the yellowjacket season, hang a small piece of fish just above the water to keep yellowjackets away. Then it would probably be a good idea to fish a yellowjacket pattern downstream after the fish had hung there for a while—no need to let all that excellent yellowjacket "chum" go to waste.

There is another variety of wasp that makes a large paper nest, which is suspended from tree limbs. On more than one occasion I have had to leave a stream because I waded too close to one of these nests near the water and the wasps didn't appreciate my presence. The rationale for using wasp patterns on the downstream side should be obvious.

I am not sure that the spider or skater patterns can fool a trout into thinking they are real spiders. Spiders are plentiful and their webs are numerous in the overhanging vegetation along a trout stream, where, I'm sure, they do a good business with aquatics that fly into their nets. I don't recall ever collecting many spiders from trout stomachs, but as I said in Chapter 12 on grasshoppers and crickets, I haven't gotten many crickets out of trout stomachs either but cricket patterns are real trout killers.

The spider and skater patterns are at their best when skimmed or skated across the surface of relatively calm waters. Since this method of working the artificial doesn't resemble any insect behavior I have observed, this tends to strengthen my belief that the skaters and spiders are attractor patterns. Whatever the appeal, they work, and a few should be on hand when you are on a stream. They are at their best—indeed, don't work well—unless they are on fine, long leaders that have been treated with leader sink.

Skaters are at their best in shallow, still waters. Fine, long leaders are also necessary for the delicate presentation of skaters, in this type of water where trout are more easily spooked than usual. It seems strange that a fly designed to be skimmed over the surface must be presented with such finesse during the cast, but that is what usually works. I believe that the type of water where this fly is usually fished contributes to the fish's being sensitive to anything but an ultra-delicate delivery. A trout has little security in still, shallow water because he has no depth for security and the smooth surface affords no concealment. This makes him extremely vulnerable to predatory birds such as kingfishers or ospreys.

If you see a fish working in the shallows, do not cast too close to him. This is a common mistake; since still waters often have subtle currents, this requires some close scrutiny to decide just where to place a skater for the proper drift. Be alert for eddies that may even flow upstream in these still waters.

In recent years beetles have gotten some well-deserved attention in the fishing journals. Gardeners and farmers hate them, but trout consider beetles to be a delicacy and will feed on them with gusto during the middle and late summer months. These crunchy terrestrials will in all probability be present in most of the trout stomachs you examine during the late summer months.

Beetles come in a wide array of sizes, and though trout are not usually too choosy about size, there are a few exceptions. On several occasions I have encountered trout that demonstrated a decided preference for beetle patterns closely resembling the size, shape, and color of Japanese beetles. The darker, dark brown, or black beetle patterns seem to be the best producers. I fish the darker hues more often than some of the more exotic colors, though, which may account for my catching more fish on these darker versions.

The heavy shells on most beetles make them poor swimmers. Since they do float for a while, if you must fish on the surface, the deer-hair beetle patterns float quite nicely. I once met a fellow fly fisherman on a stream in Tennessee and we sat down to rest and smoke our pipes together. As the discussion drifted toward fly fishing and flies he showed me a beetle pattern that was simply a piece of cork shaped to a beetle silhouette, then painted with several coats of metallic green paint used by modelmakers to paint model cars. It was more of a small cork plug than a fly pattern, but it floated well and fooled a lot of trout, though it didn't prove too durable and was soon chewed up.

Beetles are not new as models for artificials—some of the most revered angling writers have expounded on their virtues at length. Izaak Walton mentioned using live beetles for bait in his *The Compleat Angler*, published in 1676, in which the noble Piscator explains the virtues of various baits to Venator and mentions the beetle. Piscator also told where to find beetle bait: under a "cow-tird" (outdoor writers couldn't spell any better then than they can now).

The stream where this lad and his dad caught these trout long ago has become the victim of a pork-barrel dam project. To reduce such devastation, every trout fisherman should be an active member in an organization like Trout Unlimited. Photo courtesy Don Pfitzer.

Afterword

THERE ARE ONLY TWO KINDS OF TROUT FISHERMEN: those that are members of a cold-water fishery conservation group—and those that *should* be members of such groups! Organizations like Trout Unlimited (see the address on page 146) need and deserve your participation and support. If you have fished for any length of time at all you must have witnessed the destruction of some of our best cold-water fishery habitat. Urban sprawl, industrial pollution, acid rain, road construction, and unrestricted timber harvesting destroy trout streams every day.

A whole nation watched as politicians destroyed the last flowing section of the Little Tennessee River, the habitat of the endangered snail darter, in a prime example of "pork barrelmanship" instead of "statesmanship." The strongest lobbying force in Washington is said to be the National Rifle Association, which may be true, but fishermen outnumber hunters better than two to one. If anglers demonstrated the same concern for their sport that hunters do, the fishing lobby would be the strongest in the country and politicians would think twice about destroying habitat to feather their own political nests. You don't have to join, but be prepared to explain to your grandson why there are no trout left for him to enjoy!

In addition to being instrumental in conserving trout and their habitats, organizations like Trout Unlimited offer other benefits. You get to meet other anglers and share information on techniques, tackle, fly patterns, and places to fish. Many meetings feature informative programs on trout biology, fly tying, casting, and other subjects of interest to anglers.

Outdoorsmen are beginning to follow the example of tennis players and golfers by participating in schools taught by professionals. Enrollments in hunting and fishing schools have increased tremendously in recent years. Here is a partial list of some of the most respected schools:

Fenwick Fly-Casting & Angling Seminars

Eastern Division
  Jim Gilford
  2202 Glen Court
  Route 7
  Frederick, Md. 21701

Western Division
  Mel Krieger
  790 27th Avenue
  San Francisco, Calif. 94121

Midwestern Division
  Midwestern Division
  Gary Borger
  309 S. 11th Avenue
  Wausau, Wis. 54401

Kaufman's Fly Fishing Schools
P.O. Box 23032
Portland, Ore. 97223

Southeastern Outdoor Seminars
Route 1
Talking Rock, Ga. 30175

Bud Lilly's Trout Shop
P.O. Box 698
West Yellowstone, Mont. 59758

Joan and Lee Wulff Fishing School
Beaverkill Road
Lew Beach, N.Y. 12753

Orvis Fly Fishing School
Manchester, Vt. 05254

Many of the local Trout Unlimited chapters offer both fly-fishing and fly-tying schools. For the address of the nearest chapter write Trout Unlimited, P.O. Box 361, Denver, Colo. 80201.

Fishing is becoming a popular course in many schools and colleges. The American Fishing Tackle Manufacturers Association has even set up a youth education foundation to assist schools in adding fishing to the curriculum. (Information can be obtained by writing to AFTMA Youth Education Foundation, AFTMA Center, 2625 Clearbrook Drive, Arlington Heights, Ill. 60005.) The foundation has a kit that includes an outline and books for teaching the course. This program is a tremendous asset in attracting and educating the next generation of anglers.

Index